Expanding Student Assessment

by

Association for Supervision
and Curriculum Development

ASCD publications present a variety of viewpoints. The views expressed or implied in this publication are not necessarily official positions of the Association.

Printed in the United States of America.

Ronald S. Brandt, *Executive Editor*
Nancy Modrak, *Managing Editor, Books*
Julie Houtz, *Senior Associate Editor*
Ginger Miller, *Associate Editor*
Carolyn Pool, *Associate Editor*
Cole Tucker, *Editorial Assistant*
Gary Bloom, *Manager, Design and Production Services*
Stephanie Kenworthy, *Asst. Manager, Design and Production Services*
Keith Demmons, *Graphic Designer*
Valerie Sprague, *Desktop Publisher*

Price: $14.95
ASCD Stock No.: 611-91114
ISBN: 0-87120-182-8

Library of Congress Cataloging-in-Publication Information

Expanding student assessment / edited by Vito Perrone.
    p.   cm.
   Includes bibliographical references.
   ISBN 0-87120-182-8
    1. Educational tests and measurements—United States.
I. Perrone, Vito.
LB3051.E97 1991
371.2'6'0973—dc20   91-18470
                                         CIP

Expanding Student Assessment

Foreword

For many of us, the word *assessment* conjures up images of students hunched over test booklets, quietly scratching away with No. 2 pencils. From these standardized tests we receive numbers that are supposed to tell us how well our students are learning. Many educators, however, believe that such assessment tells us little about students. They believe that assessment can—and should—involve much more.

The contributors to this book have directed their energies toward finding better ways to assess student learning. In doing so, they have asked themselves the same questions that we must ask: What is the purpose of student assessment? Is it to determine whether students have learned what we expect them to learn? Is it to allow us to compare student performance from state to state or nation to nation? Or is it something more?

By asking these questions, we may find, like the authors of this book, that standardized tests given once or twice a year do not meet all our needs. They are narrow measures that don't do justice to the child as a developing person. Only by expanding our repertoire of assessments and making assessment an integral part of the educational process can we evaluate the whole child, not just his or her performance on a multiple-choice test.

The implications of expanding our assessment methods are enormous, for assessment is tied to the content of the curriculum, to what teachers do in the classroom, and to the standards we set for learning. The authors of this book challenge test makers, teachers, curriculum developers, principals, and even students, to question themselves about their educational goals and to then develop assessment methods that support these goals. They challenge us to improve children's learning, not children's test scores.

CORRINE HILL
ASCD President, 1991–92

v

Introduction

Vito Perrone

Student evaluation is basic to student growth. It demands careful, thoughtful attention. Yet what typically passes for student evaluation, what fills the public discourse, is an overarching model of assessment, built around a host of standardized tests, that doesn't get particularly close to student learning and doesn't provide teachers with much information of consequence. It is in most settings a wasteful effort that guarantees too many students a limited education and does little to increase public confidence in the schools.

In many schools, teaching to the test has become a significant part of the curriculum. And though the test facsimiles and tricks that such a process comprises may raise test scores, they are hardly the grist for an empowering education. Rising test scores are no longer matters for public celebration because they are not matched by widespread demonstrations of real competence.

Test scores in New York City, for instance, have been rising for a decade, and averages are now above national norms. But the popular view is that the city's schools are in a state of collapse, offering students too little substantial education. In fact, almost every school district in every state now reports above-average scores on most testing programs, but people generally believe that schools have made little significant, large-scale improvement.

There are indications, however, that policymakers at all levels are beginning to understand that conventional assessments reduce the decision-making potential of educators in schools and may well be negatively influencing the direction of curricular and pedagogical practices. The changing discourse is providing an opening for teachers and administrators at the local school level to develop student evaluation processes worthy of the name—processes that are rooted principally *in* instructional programs, not apart from them, and that benefit students as they inform teachers.

This book is dedicated to furthering constructive discussion about assessment and to providing concrete directions for change. Most educators call the new nonstandardized test efforts *alternative assessments,* a label that I have come to believe gives too much legitimacy to the processes currently dominating assessment in schools. I prefer *different assessments* that get closer to student learning and are related to performance and understanding. Increasingly this kind of assessment is being defined as *authentic.* The authors in this book give authentic assessment considerable attention.

Although most directions that are different from the norm are called new, much of what is being described as authentic assessment has, in fact, a larger history. The kind of recordkeeping that makes up what is currently called *documentation,* the types of work that fill a *portfolio,* and the projects that are the basis for what we now call *performance assessment* or *exhibits of learning* were common in many 19th century schools and were basic to practices in numerous early progressive schools influenced by the work of John Dewey, William Kilpatrick, Marietta Johnson, and Caroline Pratt, among others. Although the historical precedents are not fully explored here, it is important to know that some of the ground has been turned up before.

Taken together, the diverse chapters of this book outline many of the difficulties surrounding current standardized testing. Through a healthy mix of theory and practice, they present ideas that are enriching assessment activities in more and more schools every day.

Kathe Jervis, an experienced classroom teacher/ethnographer, provides a vivid picture of testing in relation to teachers and children. Although we often discuss standardized tests in terms of their technical qualities, their effects on student retention and placement, and their use for teacher and school evaluation, Jervis describes how standardized tests disrupt the normal flow of classroom practice, interfere with effective teaching and learning, and produce unnecessary, even undesirable, anxieties. For Daryl, the student who is central to her account, the disruption is educationally perilous. Many who stand far away from classrooms might view her account as extreme, but I have observed similar and even more unsettling circumstances; the story she shares has been recounted to me over and over again by teachers in every part of the United States.

Edward Chittenden engages the emerging interest in authentic assessment by suggesting, appropriately I believe, that the term needs greater definition in practice. He prefers *documentation* as a formulation within which to consider assessment, primarily because it suggests to him a diversity of assessment techniques. Chittenden works in schools where educators want to rely less on standardized testing. (He points out that schools don't typically go from testing to no testing.) His framework for assessment includes observation, performance samples, and tests (though not necessarily standardized tests). Chittenden makes a strong case for building upon the formal and informal assessment practices that teachers already use. In this particular understanding, his work makes a good connection to the work outlined by Carroll and Carini in Chapter 4.

Chittenden also raises the question of the purposes of evaluation. One problem with many standardized tests is that they don't help answer teachers' and parents' questions; they are disconnected from essential purposes.

In "Building a School Structure of High Standards," Ron Berger, an extraordinary teacher in western Massachusetts, uses *projects* as the base of his interdisciplinary curriculum. What is clear to an observer of Berger's work is that most standardized testing programs are unrelated to his classroom purposes and if made central would limit the possibilities for student learning. In Berger's classroom, the *quality* of teaching and learning are more important than the quantity, and the stress placed on high standards is inspiring. Berger's effort to match assessment to students' work represents a perspective that we need to keep in mind as we move assessment activities to higher levels of usefulness. Assessment that works should, as Berger notes, promote high-quality performance—a sense of caring about what is done.

David Carroll and Patricia Carini also bring assessment to the classroom level. They argue that teachers who work day in, day out with students know the students, understand their questions, and can address their growth as learners. Teachers who are deeply involved with their students don't need a test to know how well they read, write, or think. In describing practical ways for teachers to get close to student learning and use that knowledge to provide for ongoing learning, Carroll and Carini emphasize the importance of more fully recognizing the basic knowledge that teachers acquire from actual teaching.

The Prospect School, the setting for the work that Carroll and Carini describe, has been a pioneer in developing assessment practices that seek to make children's learning visible over time and are rooted in performance on learning tasks that children value. Over the past three decades, the school's work has given that concept particularly rich meanings.

One long-standing criticism of current standardized testing practices revolves around matters of validity—how tests relate to performance beyond the tests themselves. Is it possible that a student could score well on a language arts test and not be an effective reader or writer? Essentially, this kind of validity question expresses a desire to see whether the test actually tests what it purports to test in relation to performance in the world.

Rieneke Zessoules and Howard Gardner, drawing on their Project Zero experience, share ways in which authentic assessment has moved into the classroom. From their perspective, powerful pedagogy and curriculum lead to authentic assessment. And they make clear that teaching, learning, and assessment are, at their best, fully and necessarily reciprocal. Assessment is not, as they view it, just an end. It is a complex undertaking—always more than a simple test—that is organized to determine students' understanding, their capacity for constructing and using knowledge.

Zessoules and Gardner emphasize that classroom teachers and students are central to the development of authentic assessment, but they also make a strong case for the importance of supportive administrators' establishing the kind of context that enables such development. Everything I know about schools suggests they are correct.

Many factors have helped alter the assessment landscape, but changes in writing assessment have been most significant. While basic skills instruction was getting a boost in the 1980s because of the increased emphasis on standardized testing, a writing revolution was also taking hold. The work of the National Writing Project, with its focus on using writing as a basis for individual and shared thought and its commitment to a community of readers of writing, pushed schools to think again about how writing was taught and assessed. This revolution made clear that writing could be assessed only by reading real writing. Over time, the assessment of writing assumed a longitudinal focus, and teachers made portfolios the basis for helping students improve their writing abilities.

Patricia Stock, an experienced teacher of writing, provides a wonderfully rich account of how staying in touch with student writing affects the quality of the writing. Her description of Wendy's writing over the course of a year, along with her pedagogical use of assessment, tells an important story. There is no existing standardized test that could have created the context for writing improvement that Stock discusses.

Science teaching and learning have long suffered from their textbook quality. At best, students tend to learn *about* science; they do not experience science as an active field of inquiry, full of uncertainty and alternative explanations, open to student construction. The argument has long been that active science is not particularly amenable to the assessment models that dominate schools. George Hein makes a strong case for an active science program and describes assessment efforts that support such a direction. By drawing on examples from outside the United States (e.g., in Great Britain) as well on practice closer to home, he enriches our discussion enormously.

The secrecy that surrounds standardized testing has also been criticized for years. Judah Schwartz outlines the effect of that secrecy on assessment in mathematics, but he could as easily have been writing about science, social studies, or literature. As important as the critique, however, is his perspective about a fresh way to think about math assessment that moves to the idea of math as construction. What I especially like about Judah's work is his concern about student understanding. To speak of understanding is to go to the heart of the educational encounter.

National testing as a means of addressing accountability and determining educational progress has recently been given new life. As currently formulated, efforts to develop a national test do not promise constructive change in the schools. And they could well undermine the more productive directions that are discussed in this book and that promise more attention to student learning and curriculum as well as a level of accountability that those in schools believe has meaning.

Walter Haney, long one of our principal historians and scholarly critics of tests, even as he believes that some externally developed tests can be useful, helps us understand more fully the implications of proposals for national testing. Importantly, he places the claims of national testing, integral to the federal America 2000 proposal, within a broader historical and crosscultural context. He also sets forth suggestions about how to think more imaginatively about assessment policy, making clear that interests in accountability will not be well served by more tests.

Throughout this volume there is a strong focus on teachers and classroom practice. If we are serious about assessment, there is really nowhere else to be, for the classroom is the hub of teaching and learning. It is where we have to go if we want to get a clear picture, not a distorted image, of students' knowledge and understanding.

1

Closed Gates in a New York City School

Kathe Jervis

"Some gates are so locked up they couldn't be doorways."
—Arnie, April 19

Interrupted Rhythm

Compared with schools where tests loom large and preparation, subtle or not, starts as early as January, P.S. 135 mobilizes late. The faculty meeting agenda on April 19 casually lists testing among several items to be discussed. Otherwise, the school, just back from spring vacation, is singularly unfocused on next week's tests. It is this lack of concern about standardized tests that gives Karen (not her real name) the freedom to teach her class according to her own strong values and to reject the tests as a crucial measure of her children's achievements or her own. Karen can proceed with her 3rd–4th grade curriculum as she and the children choose. Her gift to them is time.

I spent a year in Karen's classroom as a note-taking observer. I was not a participating teacher—we agreed that I would write and she would teach. Mine was the luxurious perspective of the undistracted eye. My goal was to understand and make explicit what Karen did in the classroom. We need to know more about how individual teachers operate, how they think about children, and how their philosophy influences what they do. The observations I've recorded here will, I hope, show just how important teachers are in assessing student learning.

Author's note: This chapter is part of another book in progress. I would like to thank Patricia Carini, Diane Mullins, Vito Perrone, and Lillian Weber for their helpful comments.

From my notes, April 19:

The kids are genuinely delighted to see each other this first day back after spring vacation, especially Nick, Daryl, and Jared. All are eager to share important news with peers and grown-ups. In the first five minutes, Bill tells me about his dead gerbil and Raymond whispers in my ear that over vacation he was circumcised. As always, the first order of the day is chatting, and then there is the task of putting the room back together after the thorough vacation cleaning. The rug is gone and tables and chairs are stacked up. Karen moves individually among the children and gives them jobs, which get done with varying degrees of thoroughness. There is no suggestion that the hanging out and goofing off while doing these jobs is out of bounds. It is all very companionable.

At 9:45, Karen calls a meeting. The topic turns leisurely from Karen's reminder about setting up a tank for the classroom hermit crabs to Nick's description of his mother helping him set up a fish tank at home, then to Louise's story about how she caught and cleaned fish, and then to Jared's telling how he cooked a fish. Jeremy asks, "Has anyone eaten raw fish?" Daryl interjects a comment about how many people are killed in a year by sharks, momentarily energizing the group with the morbid image. Karen imposes no focus. This is a time to share. As she begins to write names on the board to keep track of the discussants, Celestine raises her hand and aggressively spits out, "LaFonta has something to say."

LaFonta begins hesitantly, but she gains the children's attention with her topic:

"I went down south to see my grandmother, and they shoot hogs there." She describes in detail all the "green stuff" that came out and how her grandmother said it was all gut. "When we barbecued it, it was good," she says, smiling at the memory. Karen adds that "the green stuff" is intestines, which sparks Nick to relate what he learned from a movie he saw before he was hospitalized to have his appendix out. Using his own body to demonstrate, he explains that we have two tubes, one for "pee" and one for "doo-doo."

The conversation has a relaxed tone. The children trust each other and Karen to take seriously what they say. The discussions are not always logical to an observer, but the children bring their own logic. George, or Jose as he calls himself intermittently, picks up LaFonta's story: "My grandmother hangs up a live pig from the tail and then my grandfather takes a machete and slits it down the middle. He puts a pan below to catch the guts." The discussion digresses to an exploration of the definition of "machete." Then George launches into a more precise description of how he chopped off the pig's head. He has the class hanging on every word, gesture, and sound effect. "All this happened when I was in Puerto Rico."

Jared interrupts, "You Puerto Rican?"

George/Jose of the uncertain ethnic identity says emphatically, "NO. I was born here but I was in Puerto Rico for three years." Jared is interested in further details and keeps asking questions, but George wants to talk about the pig. Karen protects him, saying, "Jared, let him finish his train of thought." Jared's patience is low to nonexistent, but he stops. Karen has done little during this discussion except protect George from Jared's incessant interruptions. The children are talking to each other, not to the teacher.

George continues. "My grandfather has about 100 acres. They filmed the killing of the pig. Then I went to my uncle's house and they stuck a stake through the pig and turned it around and around and cooked it. I got to eat the center, not the head or the tail."

Richard, who just got back from Guatemala, adds that on the slides he is going to show the class, people are killing a pig and he is helping them. They will see how different it is in Guatemala.

In the preceding minutes, three children have vividly described to a rapt audience their experiences of hog butchering in different locales and compared methods of catching blood, kinds of knives, and family roles in the ceremony. This comfortable sharing, which is also a valid social studies curriculum, thrives in a community where competitive individual effort is de-emphasized and the teacher allows time for children to become the "centrality" (Karen's word for an uncompromised first priority). This is Karen's room at its best; children telling their own stories, "appreciating" each other (Karen's word for the basic respect and pleasure one gives and gains in human interaction), and relishing the cultural differences and similarities in the group. What the system imposes interrupts the flow of life in Karen's classroom.

Standardized Tests in New York City Schools

Testing rituals mark the rhythm of the school year with the regularity of falling leaves and melting snow. For many educators, tests represent the culmination of effort, the end result of purposeful teaching, and the measure of an effective school—but not at P.S. 135. Even here, however, testing is not a fully benign event. What makes it more serious than just another bureaucratic exercise is that the testing has the power to change children's lives.

In 1980, New York City abandoned "automatic social promotion" in favor of strict measures of academic progress. The Board of Education began to use the tests to identify 4th and 7th graders who scored one year behind grade level in reading and two years behind in math. Such children failed the test, and did not pass through the "promotional Gates." They were segregated with other low-scoring children in "Gates classes" and could not be promoted to 5th or 8th grade until they passed the tests. They could retake the tests at the end of summer school, the following January, or in April. If they failed to pass again, they were assigned to a "double Gates" class.

These testing rituals mirror a society absorbed with comparing children one against another. Nowhere is the penalty more severe or the pressure greater than on children who worry about retention. For these children, the tests mean not only facing negative adult judgments about their performance, but perhaps repeating a grade and publicly being labelled a failure. Repeating a grade is not automatically terrible for every child. Careful consideration of a child's best interest may, on occasion, lead to a decision to retain a student, but when test scores alone force children to repeat a grade, children are not well served.

The pressures that low-scoring children face are damaging enough, but this reliance on tests scores puts schools in an ever-tightening vise. When tests determine what is taught, the curriculum narrows. Children are given fewer opportunities to develop their strengths and spend more time in drills for multiple-choice exams. Occasions for children's initiative are reduced. Children are encouraged to be more passive, more obedient to authority, and less enthusiastic about asking and answering open-ended questions. The "right answer" becomes the goal and children are left practicing isolated test-taking skills.

A close look at Karen's classroom during testing—a classroom in a school that values children's individuality and does not pigeonhole them according to standardized measures—illuminates both children's and teachers' responses to the heightened emotional flurry that surrounds any testing. That children are so visible in Karen's classroom increases the opportunity to observe what each child thinks and feels about tests.

Kids who test well, test essentially the same way; kids who test badly, test badly in their own way. The academically high-powered in this class (Marion, Susanna, Tony, and Raymond) have already learned how to take tests. These children face years of test taking, which will sort them into high-level school tracks, perhaps even win them college scholarships. They already have the skills, the stamina, and the self-confidence to succeed. Children with *certified* learning difficulties (Jeremy and Bill), non-middle class minority children (Jared, Nick, and Daryl), and those children whose first language is not English (Asfid and Theresa), make up the bottom of the scale. For them, tests mean anxiety, pressure, and potential failure. Thus, the tests interfere with Karen's efforts to build these students' self-confidence.

Observing children is Karen's route to understanding. She believes that "once I know a child, I can see the learning in what the child has chosen to do in the classroom, and the activities become more legitimate to me as the teacher. Children usually can't articulate their vital concerns. When I see what their questions are, then I can help them recognize what they are about. The more I know children, the better I can provide for their learning." Karen's observations yield more knowledge about children than any standardized test scores. She does not need these narrow measures to confirm what she knows or to dictate the content of her teaching. Every teacher is caught in the same bind. Karen has no choice but to test. Undermining her usual teaching style, the tests drain her energy and the tension shows.

A Stab at Preparation

When the class returns from recess, Karen introduces her only effort at formal test preparation. She retrieves two faint ditto sheets from a file folder and asks the children to gather on the rug. Laconic in speech and rich in gesture, Karen says to the children, "Get a fake test and figure out what to do," dramatically sweeping her hand toward a pile on a nearby table. "Don't ask for help," she adds. Her children, used to gathering their own supplies, filling up blank pages without publishing companies' suggestions, and generally making sense of their world by imposing their own structure, are rarely constrained so thoroughly as by these "fake tests." Most go to it, picking up a paper and settling themselves to work on the floor or at large tables. The novelty entices the children and they're momentarily engaged, except for those who are academically vulnerable; they don't know where to begin.

Instructions in the upper-right-hand corner of this standardized practice sheet advise the teacher in less-than-elegant prose that:

> The first four questions on this starter force awareness that the right answer may be in any position. The wrong choices of the other

questions can be studied with the students in order to alert them to the different kind of "distractors" this format most frequently uses.

In slightly larger print, the child is asked to choose one of four words, which "makes the sentence most true." Twelve everyday phrases can be completed by selecting the proper word. But this exercise is not straightforward for every child.

Asfid, despite her improving spoken English, reads and writes only in her native Arabic. The fake test makes no more sense than the real one will, but as this is Asfid's third year at P.S. 135, no dispensation is forthcoming. Karen does not do what some teachers are reputed to do: hint that Asfid should stay home in order not to lower the class and school average. Asfid attends school only at Karen's urging; girls in Asfid's family take the veil at twelve and retreat into the world of women and home. Asfid, who has just turned twelve, is needed to care for a newly arrived sixth child, but Karen has prevailed on the family to let her stay in school. Unless her parents reverse themselves, Asfid will not be in school next year.

I am sitting near Jared as he reads aloud. I am the ostensible audience, but he is really reading for himself. He is frozen in place and his body is stiff as he holds the paper at an awkward distance. Barely able to decode the instructions, he is too tense to figure out what the test is asking him to do. I am tempted to tell him to ignore the directions because they are more difficult than the actual task, but before I do, Jared remedies his own discomfort by leaving for the bathroom. Academically, he is the weakest of the English-speaking children and temperamentally the most nervous about the tests.

I nagged Karen frequently about Jared. I felt he needed daily reading instruction not only in order to pass the test, but to learn to read. Karen's answer never changed: "He has been in too many schools for his short life. Every time he has an academic problem, his parents change his school. What Jared needs is a 'house' [Karen's word for parental attention]. He needs his mother to see him sometime between 3:00 p.m. and midnight. What he does not need is my white female body standing over him everyday reminding him what he can't do.

"You know," she never ceased to remind me, "Jared doesn't come from a family of books. He needs time to find books pleasurable, to ease into reading gently and socially. Besides, he hasn't done so well with other teachers' daily reading lessons."

Jeremy, labelled dyslexic by the Committee on the Handicapped, receives intensive help every day in the Resource Room. He reads through the directions word-for-word without the rhythm of understanding. That he even approaches this paper-and-pencil job is a sign of growth. The adults have confidence that Jeremy will do well enough on the tests because his reading is progressing smoothly, but his palpable anxiety may interfere more than anyone expected. He is chewing a big wad of gum. "Ditch it," says Karen. He goes to the trash returning with the gum obviously in his mouth. She nods to him to get rid of it and he comes back with the gum barely concealed in his hand. Jeremy's uncharacteristic noncompliance is a stark reminder of the pressure on a learning-to-read child faced with reading tasks that matter to the important adult in his life. His mother, a single parent for almost his whole life, is nearly beside herself because her only child is not a fluent reader. Someday he might be a famous architect because his spatial sense is so highly refined, or he might capitalize on his incredible ability to interpret captionless political cartoons or draw intricate cartoons of his own, but right now his limited reading skill looms so large that it obscures his strengths. Only his intransigence and his anger are visible.

On the other hand, Arnie works at a good pace, talking about why he chose one answer over another. He is wrong in most cases, but his reasons are good. I file away a prediction that his scores will be lower than his reading ability merits. He is one of the thinking test takers who defeat themselves by looking too far below the surface of the questions and answers. In no danger of failing, he only risks disappointing his parents, who expect stellar scores. Most students are like Louise, Marion, and Susanna; they are doing the sheet just as they usually do their regular work, with good humor and enjoyment, and—despite Karen's instructions—looking up answers in the dictionary and discussing them as they go along. The tests hold no special meaning for them; they are merely a break in the routine. Others, especially Daryl and Celestine, do not attract attention during this practice session, but Karen predicts the test will be a strain regardless of their academic abilities because they can't play the game of institutional compliance required of test takers.

Twenty minutes after starting, Karen says, "Everyone come sit on the rug," and from her sitting position on the floor indicates that discussing the answers is going to be a group exercise. The one-correct-answer format is rare for these children in matters of language and they are finding it an enjoyable novelty. Some of them continue to fill in answers while a child volunteers to read the question. The only clue that this is anything other than routine busywork is the alacrity with which Karen jumps on noisy children. As usual, she does not address the entire class, but draws children into the group individually. She says calmly, "If you disagree with an answer, say so."

The exercise continues uneventfully until number six: "A gate is a (a) doorway (b) climb (c) swing (d) garden." Nick answers, "Swing," because you could swing on a gate if you wanted. Jason says, "Doorway," and Arnie, the thinker, proposes, "Some gates are so locked up they couldn't be doorways." In one of her rare interventions, Karen retorts, "So what does the TESTMAKER want?" Marion, the consummate test taker, says, "It really isn't a doorway, but that is the best answer." Louise adds, "A gate isn't a doorway, but that is the best answer. A gate is outside and a doorway isn't, and anyway, you don't say, 'Shut the doorway,' but you say, 'Shut the gate.'" Still she admits, "'Doorway' is the best answer," thus resolving the question for herself if not for Arnie.

The next snag is at number twelve: "Geese are a type of (a) gull (b) fowl (c) hen (d) swan." Arnie is sparked. He looks up "geese" in the dictionary but the answer still eludes him. The lunch bell rings. Karen motions for everyone to stay. Arnie looks up every one of the choices, but absolutely resists "fowl." Jared is jumping out of his skin with irritation. "*You* brought your lunch, *you* don't have to stand in line," he says angrily to Arnie. Karen ignores him. She suggests to Arnie that nothing fits except "fowl" because the form of the question, "geese are," requires a plural answer and "fowl" is the only possibility. Arnie doesn't see it that way. He insists that perhaps a gull or a swan is a kind of goose, and would have gone on with his idea but for his classmates' noisy lack of interest in this post-lunch-bell disputation. Karen dismisses the class and they all leave for lunch—even agitated Arnie.

Karen storms at me, "Why are we putting such energy into this? These tests stink." Karen routinely rails against the system, which uses tests to rank kids according to their proficiency on multiple-choice test items, some of which are ambiguous at best, and culturally biased at worst. It makes her furious to think that decisions about kids' futures are going to be made based on this narrow conception of learning in which half the population is always below the mean.

She stomps in to lunch, which doubles today as a monthly faculty meeting, only to find the lunch table littered with copies of Board of Education Memo #108: TEST SECURITY MUST BE ABSOLUTE. The teachers, eager to chat this Monday after vacation, pay no attention to the memo. The questions about testing are buried in the third item on the principal's agenda, and are quickly resolved. Only three teachers take the memo as they leave.

The tests bring an unexpected bonus at the end of the week: a school-sanctioned holiday. Friday afternoon is designated a "clerical half-day" and children are released from school early to give teachers time to prepare the answer sheets. Two years ago, children were thought to be capable of filling in their age, birthday, grade, and sex, but as testing has become a more serious matter, the Board has the teachers perform this clerical job in order to ensure eradication of every error. Filling out the machine-coded "bubbles" does not take teachers all of this gorgeous Friday afternoon, and after an hour and twenty minutes, the teachers are in a congenial mood as they leave to enjoy the spring sunshine. The tests will begin on Monday.

Atmospheric Pressure

The Monday morning air is heavy with humidity, which will shortly turn to rain. Friday's sunshine would have been a welcome mood lightener. The dark sky gives Karen's room a gloomy feel.

As always, Louise arrives first. She is wearing huge, adult-looking cowboy boots; their weighty clunk combined with her controlled dancer's gait results in an odd, idiosyncratic noise wherever she goes. Today she teeters on her heels every third step, which echoes loudly in the empty room. This is her only outer sign of nervousness. Louise has nothing to fear; her confidence is high, her middle-class background is a plus for successful test taking, and she has reasonably good skills. She stops next to Karen, squinting and wrinkling her nose while she reads various messages on the board. Most children, like Louise, take the tests in stride. Not Nick.

Nick comes in, takes one look at the board and insists, "No, no, no. I don't want no reading tests, please." Nick is a black child from a poor, working-class background whose lively personality conceals his history of rock-bottom test scores. He moves with the grace of an athlete or a dancer. He is both. Last year he was given a prestigious ballet school scholarship but he gradually became less involved and finally dropped out. In his fourth year at P.S. 135, he is repeating 3rd grade. According to his last teacher, his oral and written skills "are the weakest possible." In September, he rarely spoke and, when he did, he was hard to understand. Karen was unsure whether he was really mumbling, was speaking a variation of black English, or had a more serious impediment. She almost had him tested, which would have been an extreme act on her part, but as he relaxed in her class he spoke more clearly and more often.

Recently, everyone was reminded how dramatically Nick has improved when Daryl editorialized during a meeting, saying, "Nick, he always be tellin' his stories." But while Nick's speech has improved, basic schoolwork is still hard for him; he lacks the persistence and stamina for intellectual endeavors, as well as the discipline for rigorous ballet instruction.

In an ideal world, Nick's family would provide the support for developing his verbal skills and insist he continue with dance. Karen sees one of her roles as providing this support, which she believes is accomplished by nurturing children's self-esteem. "Nick is feeling good and standing taller," Karen says about his giant strides, and it pains her that the tests are likely to deflate his growing confidence. Karen desperately wants to save him (and others) from a school career in the lowest tracks, a fate that undoubtedly awaits him beyond heterogeneously grouped P.S. 135. Karen maintains the only viable way to extricate children from this self-defeating cycle of low scores and low tracks is to help them become supremely confident about their abilities. Nick is making progress by Karen's standards, but his academics are not yet secure enough that he approaches the tests with confidence. Rather, the tests are an unwelcome reminder that others are considerably more skilled than he is. Abandoning his usual physical ease, Nick darts here and there as he moves stiffly to find some peer support, but his friends are still at breakfast.

The room is filling up now. Unlike most days, there is tension in the air. The room is noisy. Those children who anticipate doing well view the testing as a welcome break in the schedule. Others are tense because they fear the consequences or because they are anxious about school performance. Dawn is temperamentally one of these children. She erupts into the room as if from nowhere, immediately making her presence felt. In a shrill voice she announces to no one in particular, "I studied all weekend. I couldn't even go roller skating. My father and mother wouldn't let me. It's all your fault." This last comment is directed to Karen, who says nothing and gestures good morning with a nod of her head. Dawn approaches Nick, who is still standing by the door, and asks him, "Do you want the math test or the reading test first?"

"I don't want no tests," he says warily. Dawn interrupts this conversation to act as self-appointed purveyor of the testing news. She rushes around telling everyone, "The test is today," as if it were dirty gossip. In addition to her surface anxiety, Dawn is wearing clothes that add to an appearance of uneasiness: a white, lacy, short-sleeved acetate blouse and a knee-length navy sheath skirt. It is a slim teenager's outfit, but Dawn's oversized body fills out every inch, giving her the look of an overstuffed sausage. As she passes by me she stops for an instant, "Teach me math. Right now." I suggest she relax, though that is clearly impossible.

George/Jose comes through the door and checks out the room with one sweep of his eyes, settling first on Nick, whose plea for no test he must have absorbed subliminally. "Are we going to have the tests?" he questions in an urgent voice. Without waiting for an answer, he begins a constant stream of conversation. Against Karen's explicit rules, he has brought an open orange juice carton up from breakfast, which he ostentatiously waves while repeating his question from twenty feet away. Moving closer and lining up his arms next to hers, he asks, "Hey, how come your arms are so pink?"

"I got too much sun in the Forty Mile Bike Marathon. Would you please take your body and your orange juice out in the hall until you finish it." Making no move to leave with his juice, he chatters on about his own bicycle and his own caramel-colored skin compared with Karen's fair, but slightly sunburned, skin. Talking at twice his normal speed, he dumps the half-full juice carton in the trash and attaches himself like a leech to Karen while she surveys the room. This is not the poised child who captivated the class with stories about his grandfather and hog butchering. Nor is it the macho teenager who tantalizes his classmates with tales of his sexual and streetcorner exploits. He is genuinely terrified about the tests.

George/Jose is the victim of an unclear promotion policy, a casualty of a kind of problem opposite that caused by an arbitrary system. New to P.S. 135, he is repeating 4th grade, but not in a Gates class. His previous scores, so close to grade level, suggest that he was held back as a punishment for either difficult behavior or refusal to work. Both are plausible explanations. He has a short memory and a short fuse. An inadvertent jostle provokes an angry response, and a reprimand generates inappropriate back talk. Rules are broken five minutes after the last punished infraction. He isn't quite sure who he is; he is George sometimes, Jose others. His mature, well-developed body and changing voice stand out against the younger looking children in Karen's class. His skills are more than adequate, but having failed once, he has reason to be tense. He is trouble.

Daryl makes his appearance late and without ceremony. He approaches Karen: "Do we have to take the test today? Do we have to?

I don't want to." His tone is whiny and insistent. "Yes, you have to take the test," Karen says firmly. He continues to plead and Karen, purposely not getting caught up in this conversation, turns her attention elsewhere. Having made contact with her, he announces with renewed energy, "I'm going to draw until we have to take the tests." He slides onto a bench and opens his ever-ready drawing book. Among other things, Daryl is learning how to regulate himself. His ability to retreat into his drawing rather than put on a public display is a healthy development. Testing, however, is an institutional task that Daryl still cannot tolerate. No matter how skilled he is in daily classroom work, scoring one year below grade level in math on this test will require another year in 4th grade. With his record on standardized tests, no appeal would be granted—he has stood on the borderline for promotion every year.

Karen has made no general announcements about the tests. She answers questions patiently and clearly, explaining the same information as often as necessary to satisfy the children. But she waits for children to approach her individually. She makes an overture to only one child. Jared, who has a low tolerance for even Karen's loose classroom routines, is a wreck. The test has hung over him like a guillotine blade all year. His father has promised him a new pair of shoes if he gets promoted and a whipping if he doesn't. Karen now asks him, "How was your weekend?" He mumbles that he babysat his younger sister and didn't even go outside. Karen has recently sensed a change in his behavior and suspects an absence of parental attention. On Monday mornings his thoughts are scattered and his inability to focus has been a drain on the class. Karen's intuition turns out to be right; Jared's father moved out last week. His parents' separation weighs heavily on him and has become mixed with his very real anxiety over the test. He is not so much in need of new shoes as he is of his father's approval. Karen appreciates the depth of his fear and her overtly maternal gestures are meant to put him at ease.

Karen arranges seating to accommodate the larger numbers coming to her room for the test. She motions to Louise and Dawn to help move a bench. There is a book on the bench. Dawn swings her arm and with a fierce swoop sends the book crashing to the floor. Karen observes the disturbance, but ignores it. On top of the noisy tension, Dick asks Karen for the fishnet because, "I think the fish is dead." Karen groans. A bad omen? Dick disposes of the fish without comment. Right now Karen is as even-tempered as she will be all week.

The Test

Fourth graders from other classes file in and look for places to sit. Karen asks, "Who wants to sit alone?" George/Jose raises his hand and Karen points to a chair away from the group. She offers another invitation to "sit where you want." Then in a louder voice she says, "You must be quiet now." The room is noisy.

Karen makes some minor seating adjustments. Where there is choice, Karen allows it. "As long as you keep your body still, you may sit there," she tells Arnie, whose table is crowded. Twenty-eight children in self-chosen, sex-segregated seats are waiting to begin the first test.

The children in Karen's class have had virtually no experience with testing during this year. Their practice has been gearing up for the concentrated bursts of energy useful in pursuing their own interests. High-adrenalin activities run counter to the low-key calm to which Karen accustoms her class. Her children have been neither evaluated against any uniform standard nor ranked against each other. They are used to helping their friends and expect that adults will help them if they need it. They do not work in silence, nor do they ever labor under a time limit. Testing differs from this norm in every significant aspect. Although scores might—just might—be higher if children were exposed to more test conditions, Karen feels strongly that her usual atmosphere of noncompetition, community effort, and relaxing pace benefits children's progress along different, if less measurable, dimensions. She believes with unwavering conviction that if she enables children to develop confidence in their own abilities, their academic skills will grow naturally and developmentally as they read and write in school.

Karen's views determine her test-giving manner. She does not rationalize the tests to the children; she just follows the rules. She does not, as some teachers do, exhort children to an abstract excellence: "Do your very best." Nor does she remind them of the consequences: ". . . or you'll be held back." She doesn't persuade children: "Try hard, but don't worry because these tests are only for the teacher's information." Her manner is matter-of-fact, but it is unmistakable that she wants the testing finished as soon as possible.

The children are ready, but not quiet. She distributes the test booklets and only when she begins to read the directions does the class cease talking. Karen calls on Celestine to read the sample question. "No," Celestine mumbles, but Karen doesn't hear and asks again. This "no" is more defiant. Allegra, a child from another class, volunteers and answers correctly. LaFonta reads the second sample and Karen gives the signal to begin. This vocabulary test is like the practice sheet done in class. The hardest question is a synonym for "accept," as in "Accept the prize." The choices are: (a) see (b) earn (c) take (d) want. The children get right to work. But it is clear Celestine is going to be a problem.

Celestine has not left the room screaming for months, but the test situation triggers an old uncooperativeness. She has one thumb over her eyeball, and is pushing her eyelid back to reveal the whole white, in the process letting her glance fall on Dawn's paper. Dawn, already on the verge of hysteria, complains loudly, "Celestine's looking." To which Karen calmly replies, "Celestine, look at your own paper." "I am," Celestine protests. She certainly is not doing the test. She chatters at LaFonta, who ignores her. Within minutes she has wound herself up almost out of control. Visibly raging, her face contorted, she makes loud noises with her mouth. Allegra raises her hand to complain and Celestine orders her to "shut up." Celestine raises her own hand. Karen comes over.

"What is it?"

"NOTHING!" is Celestine's answer. Celestine has gum, which Karen ignores.

Karen tells her bluntly, "You can't do this during a test. You've got to help out kids who have a hard time with tests." Celestine's skills are more than adequate, though she is not yet convinced of her own worth and valuable contributions to the class.

"I'm just going like this," she demonstrates noisily.

Karen insists, "You've got to be quiet." Only three children at Celestine's table are engaged by this disturbance. Karen directs their focus away from Celestine by making a general announcement: "Look for directions where it calls for opposites."

Close to the end of thirty questions and thirty minutes, Karen says, "When you are finished, close your book or check your answers." No child goes back to check. Celestine is still exercising her mouth. She blows spit at Allegra, who objects. Celestine tells her to shut up.

Karen, deliberately ignoring Celestine's bid for attention, says, "Time's up. You have a choice of going straight on or stretching." Some kids stretch. Celestine continues to annoy Allegra. Karen unceremoniously moves Allegra to a different table and motions Dawn to move to the end of the table. This new configuration gives Celestine space on either side without requiring direct confrontation or an acknowledgement of her responsibility for the necessary changes. It is not Karen's method to engage in verbal argument with Celestine or to rub her nose in misbehavior.

The next test section is reading comprehension. Karen asks Daryl to read the sample. "Ralph is late and bumped his knee on the table," he reads fluently, adding the editorial comment, "Clumsy." Defying the rules of testing, he opens the test booklet and protests yet again, "I don't want to read this story. It's too long."

"Neither do I," chimes in George/Jose. Karen gives the signal to begin the increasingly long paragraphs followed by progressively more difficult questions. The children begin working, even Celestine.

The principal is making rounds to see how everything is going. The silence is absolute. He leaves and shuts the door. Karen, who insists on teaching with an open door, walks over and opens it. A school messenger comes in to deliver a message, shutting the door as she leaves. Karen opens it again. This is the equivalent of pacing the floor.

Fifteen minutes into the test Daryl goes to the bathroom and when he comes back he moves his test booklet to another table, a sign of general restlessness. George/Jose has also moved. One senses that both these children have come to the end of their testing tolerance for the day.

The other children are quiet, but body language conveys more than silence. Though his body is relaxed and he has one leg up on the bench, Jason is biting his lip ferociously. Dick is pulling on his ear with one hand while sitting on the other, yawning as he reads. Dawn is jerking her shoulders as if she had a gross tic while she rocks her chair back and forth. Celestine flits like a hummingbird—her mouth, head, and whole body move faster than the eye can follow. No part of her is still. Not all children are somatically involved. Arnie, who loves tests, is intent, his body solidly planted on the bench. LaFonta moves quickly, with interest and a quality of alertness she brings to her work. Theresa, from Portugal, who has been in America only five months, looks relaxed enough, demonstrating what we already know—she's more secure in her written language skills than in her speech. Though she is not yet fluent enough to pass this test, she is having a good time.

Asfid, who reads no English at all, is the first one to finish. She whispers in Karen's ear that she wants to go to the movies. Somehow Asfid has found out that *Mary Poppins* is being shown in the auditorium. Karen certainly has not announced it. Karen smiles with pleasure at Asfid's secret source of information and dismisses her with a small hand gesture. As more children finish, Karen reminds each of them to check their answers. No child does. She sends them off individually to the movie, which is meant to keep children occupied until everyone is finished. Only three children remain in Karen's room: George/Jose, who is restless and no longer concentrating; Daryl, who has gone to the bathroom several times and changed his seat each time he returned; and Theresa, who is just proceeding slowly through the test. George leaves; then Theresa. Daryl is the last one finished. He is still squirming in his seat when children straggle back.

Karen decides to take the class to the gym "to rest." I follow, but as I pass the school office, the testing coordinator, frantic with administrative details, asks me to supervise two children whose cases are special enough to warrant extra time for test completion. These children failed to score high enough last year to be promoted to 5th grade and are repeating 4th grade in a Gates class. Thirteen-year-old Dwayne, held back twice already, and Jordan, an adopted child whose age is unknown, are both attempting to negotiate the 4th grade promotional gate; but, like Arnie's gates that are "so locked up they couldn't be doorways," this test presents an insurmountable obstacle.

I do not know Dwayne, who appears earnest and cooperative about settling down to finish the reading test. Jordan, on the other hand, has a schoolwide reputation. Gravelly voiced and physically mature, Jordan for years has made only rocky academic progress, but his steady growth this year has inspired his teacher's confidence that he will pass to the next grade. Jordan, however, has given up any pretense of completing the test. Full of wisecracks and bravado about how he doesn't care, he stares at the ceiling, his pencil behind his ear, his ability to read temporarily disengaged from his anxious self.

Mindful that appeals to the school district are rare and often fruitless in such cases, I am watching right under my own eyes a child's opportunities narrow, not because he can't read, but because he can't summon the stamina to complete this standardized task, which taps into his weaknesses and ignores the progress he has made. I am paralyzed with helplessness. In the hall I see the teacher who has given him daily help for years. I tell her my dilemma and she says, "I *know* he can pass this test and I'm upset he won't try. Let me supervise." Knowing Jordan has a better chance of succeeding with a familiar person, I leave. When the testing coordinator passes me in the hall on my way to the gym, she raises her eyebrows. I explain who is with the children and she replies with a scowl, "She'll help them too much." I relax.

Karen and I go out for lunch. She complains of muscle tension in her neck. We exchange not a word during our meal.

After lunch the room is damp and chilly and the rain is hard. During silent reading, LaFonta and Celestine both complain about feeling sick. For months, Celestine has not been as disruptive as she was this morning. They huddle together under LaFonta's coat where their intimate friendship regenerates Celestine's feelings of belonging to this once-alien community. Karen pays loving attention to Jared. Wordlessly she motions him to come to her. She kneels down—he is still standing, taller than anyone in the class, his comb sticking out of his back pocket ever ready to rearrange his afro, which is kept so short as to defy any attempt to change it—and ties his shoe. Her smile and gesture represent a crucial connection between them. Her unobtrusive realization of his need for mothering conveys silent support.

Karen says, "I want you to write in your logs about the test. How you felt."

Nick hears "fail" for "felt." "How are we s'posed to know if we fail?" he wails in a frightened voice. Karen repeats her instruction. He relaxes. Karen asks him, "Were you scared—before or after the test?"

"All the time, ever since last week," he answers.

Dawn adds, "I was petrified."

Jeremy, who earlier said the test was a boring waste of time, now admits with real venom in his voice, "I hated it." Then Jeremy puts his coat on to go home though there are still 35 minutes before dismissal. Karen asks him to take off his coat and write. He sits for 15 minutes, drawing a beautiful heading with his name and date and an intricate "T" for today and nothing else.

The group reverts to its usual unpressured life, though there is more noise than on a normal afternoon. Karen attributes the heightened emotions to the test and to the fact that the children have not had a typical Monday morning. "Monday morning got pushed to Monday afternoon," she observes.

The first day of testing is over. There are still three more. None will be as difficult as the first day. But all are tension-filled for Karen and for many of the children.

Aftermath

Friday morning it seems as if the tests never happened. There is a birthday message on the board for LaFonta and an assignment to identify six geographical locations, given their longitude and latitude. The children are even more unhurried than usual. Except for matter-of-fact reminders to Jared and Susanna, Karen does not push anyone to "get on with the map stuff," though she says to George/Jose, with only the mildest sarcastic tinge, "George, are you going to do any work today?" She moves calmly through the morning, cleaning the debris off her desk, showing every child individually how to put one finger on the proper latitude and another on the given longitude and move them until they meet. She also takes the temperature of the fish tank, and chats with three teachers who drop in to tell her about their vacation plans and health problems.

LaFonta's dance is the only nonroutine event. After recess, LaFonta takes center stage looking great in a purple dress, made as a gift by her sister, and a new afro barretted along one side with several clips perpendicular to her neck. The attentive class applauds her *Forty-Second Street* performance and even laughs at Celestine, who cleverly mimics the dance, calling it "Forty Stupid Street." Karen remains neutral about Celestine's funny, but unauthorized, bid for attention. When Celestine's sideshow is over, Karen reminds the group that, after lunch, two of her friends are coming from northern Massachusetts to visit.

When Karen's friends arrive, the class has 45 minutes left until dismissal with no specific expectations. One of Karen's friends, a 4th grade teacher, remarks on how relaxed this room is for a Friday afternoon. She also wonders where the purpose is in all this free time. I couldn't give a good answer then, but now I understand that Karen was restoring children to their own rhythm. The purpose of the day was to reestablish the calm and repair the damage.

The following Monday morning children make no mention of the event that was such a big deal a week ago, but the tests linger in the teachers' consciousness like an unfinished crossword puzzle that has no available answers. The Board has promised the scores on Friday, May 28th, four weeks after the last test, but the scores do not arrive, and nerves are on edge as Memorial Day weekend begins.

At about 11:00 the following Tuesday morning, I hear that the scores are in the principal's office and meander down, thinking that because teachers are in class I can satisfy my own curiosity. I am wrong. Already teachers have slipped away from their classes to get the news. The scene is ludicrous; I hardly believe I am participating. On the principal's desk is a half-finished list of high and low scores. Draped over his empty chair are ten-foot-long computer printouts that resemble unravelled paper towels. The results of the entire school are attached, and teachers form a line that quickly becomes an active semi-circle as they each reach for a piece of the number-filled paper strip. Looking at a particular class is difficult; scores are solidly printed with no divisions, and trying to find an individual's name in any orderly manner is impossible. Healthy group spirit prevails, and teachers restrain themselves: no paper is torn, nor is anyone elbowed aside, but they shriek loudly over individual children's successes and undistinguished showings. The most affect is reserved for two children who unexpectedly fail.

No matter how insignificant a place tests occupy in the philosophical terrain teachers have mapped out for themselves, it is hard to separate children's scores from teacher's performances. These teachers know high scores do not necessarily reflect their own teaching, but rationality dissipates in the face of all the excitement about these magic numbers.

P.S. 135 teachers are not competitive—decidedly the reverse—but momentary comparisons run through their responses like lumps in an otherwise smooth sauce. "Look at all the high scores in Layla's class," someone says. "She really teaches those kids." (I remember when I taught those kids last year in Karen's class they scored just as high. This group has been scoring at the top since they began school.) Logic is forgotten as the whole room is swept up by the false certainty that quantification promotes. Amidst all this chaotic euphoria and dejection, I can't get a fix on how Karen's class fared. I will have to wait until the principal officially distributes the scores. Karen certainly won't ask for them. She is the only teacher who stays away from this frenzied scene.

Karen has been amazingly consistent: She refuses to emphasize the tests during the year, gives them back with barely disguised distaste, and pays no attention to the results. Karen's teaching is based on detailed, astute, daily observations of each child and she resents this expensive, time-consuming effort that yields no useful knowledge to help her teach.

Once the initial triumph and disappointment wear off, the scores take on a life of their own, surfacing in casual conversation until they become as much a part of a child's identity as hair color or height. Karen engages in no discussion of the results. When the principal distributes the scores, Karen glances over them to see if any 4th grader failed. (No English-speaking child did.) She later dutifully affixes the computer-generated sticky labels to each child's cumulative record, noting ironically, "These test scores are the most obvious, easy-to-read information on the child's permanent record."

While I copied the test information from the cumulative records, Karen hovered around me, grumbling over my shoulder that even entering the scores in my notes "gave them too much credence." In this tense atmosphere, I put the scores away, thinking them perfectly respectable, but unremarkable. Excepting the Arabic and Portuguese speakers and Daryl, all 4th graders met the national norms in reading. But when I looked at the scores while writing this chapter, I was astounded at the 4th graders' growth: Daryl's California Achievement Test score improved the least of any English-speaking 4th grader and he moved from the 26th percentile to the 42nd percentile in reading. The average growth was 23½ percentiles.

Two weeks later, on the afternoon of June 18th, Karen tells everyone to come sit on the rug with pencils and graph paper. She teaches a lesson on perimeter. Jared is wildly eager to be chosen to give the answer for figure ABCDEF. Nick says, "You better be right or you done all that jumpin' for nothin'." Jared is wrong, but the warm class feeling generates a good-natured laugh. Karen brings them back as she points to the numbers she has written on the board. "These are your math test scores. Pick the one you want or that you think you have."

3rd	4th
99+	97
99+	83
96	69
96	61
93	56
92	55
92	54
92	44
86	30
69	11
54	
40	
30	

"I want 97," yells out George/Jose.

"That's right. That's you," says Karen.

George/Jose responds with contempt and disbelief, "Bullshit."

Karen nods with restrained approval. "That's your score."

George/Jose, quickly divorcing himself from any success, speculates, "Maybe 97 is not the highest, maybe 11 is the best."

Jared interrupts, "Arnie got 99."

Nick, thinking fast, says, "But he's not in 3rd grade so he couldn't have 99."

The kids listen attentively as Karen tells them, "The scores mean if you have a 97, then for every hundred kids who took the test, you did better than 97 kids. It does not tell you about your work, but about how you take tests and what you know." She points to the 11: "It means this person doesn't take tests well or maybe doesn't do the work in school." She starts to do some arithmetic with the number lists, soliciting the answers from the class, and concludes that 83 percent of the 3rd graders did better than the 50th percentile. "So," she says emphatically, "the 3rd graders did better than the 4th graders. Why?"

Dick suggests, "Maybe the test was easier?"

Karen nods, "Maybe. I wouldn't do very well. Some people take tests better than I do. It doesn't mean they are smarter than I am . . ." and her voice trails off. That ends the subject of tests.

The children have absorbed Karen's indifference. They do not clamor for their own scores or object when Karen suddenly moves on to another topic. Dropping the tests totally, she asks about the movie the kids watched at the library this morning, "What did the mother in *Free to Be You and Me* wish for?"

"A good friend," Marion answers.

"Can you think of anything better?" Karen asks rhetorically. And then, switching abruptly, "Rosa, when do you cry?"

"When I'm hurt," Rosa answers.

"When I'm upset," Susanna adds.

Jared adds, "When my father whips me."

Karen reveals her own answers. "I cried when I went on the Thousand Cranes March for Peace last week. I cried because I was proud. Tom cried, too."

"The principal cried?" exclaimed the class.

"Well, maybe not with tears, but he was touched that people in this school do that job of making peace in the world," says Karen, returning to her most deeply felt themes: friendship, the capacity to be touched or to appreciate when others are touched (which she often describes as crying), and the responsibility to make peace, not only in the world, but in the community. "Go get your work done." She dismisses the class.

That discussion ends the testing rituals in Room 312, but the public discussion has just begun. The *New York Times* will print these scores in a front-page story. Realtors will use them to advise their clients where to live. And university researchers will use them to identify effective schools.

2

Authentic Assessment, Evaluation, and Documentation of Student Performance

Edward Chittenden

For the past few years we have been working with educators in school districts in the New Jersey and New York area to examine assessment alternatives in elementary education. In these schools, teachers and administrators are investigating a variety of approaches to evaluating children's learning. While some of the approaches can be considered "new"—in the sense that they reflect contemporary research—the investigation of alternatives is equally a matter of taking stock of current teaching practices in order to capitalize upon assessment opportunities inherent in the classroom. As one teacher expressed it, "I don't really need a lot of new data about the children—rather I need better ways of using what I have."

In large part, the interest in assessment options has been prompted by curriculum reform in the districts. For example, teachers in many of the schools are broadening their approaches to reading instruction along the lines of "whole language" or "developmentally appropriate" practice. Greater emphasis is placed upon purposes and meaning of reading with less specific emphasis on isolated subskills. More attention is given to responding to children's interests and styles of learning, with less strict adherence to a prescribed sequence. As teaching practices change in these more open, child-oriented directions the gap between the "lessons" of instruction and the content of traditional tests becomes wider.

Author's note: Work described in this chapter has been supported by a grant from the Bruner Foundation. The text was part of a presentation made at the California ASCD Symposium on April 4–5, 1990.

Assessment interest have also been prompted by accountability concerns, especially the need for organizing the data of the classroom in ways that are credible and comprehensible to all constituencies—student, teacher, parent, and community.

Much of the work in the schools has centered on portfolios and related techniques that highlight student work and performance as the core data of assessment. As districts cut back on their use of conventional achievement tests, these work-sample approaches constitute a tangible step in designing alternatives intended to promote a better alignment of assessment and instruction. There is much variation among districts in the particular features of these alternatives but the goals seem constant: namely, to implement assessment practices that (a) capitalize on the actual work of the classroom, (b) enhance teacher and student involvement in evaluation, and (c) meet some of the accountability concerns of the district.

Although interest in assessment is widespread, progress in establishing viable alternatives has been uneven. One difficulty is that naturalistic assessment approaches entail new roles for teachers and students in the process of evaluation; thus, much more is required than simply replacing one type of instrument with another. For example, provisions must be made to bring staff together around central questions of design of assessment and standards for interpretation of data. Involvement of this sort has no counterpart in conventional achievement testing programs. In keeping with the national literature on assessment, the options being developed in these districts could variously be described as "authentic," "alternative," or as "performance measures," depending upon preference. But it needs to be noted that these terms are essentially placeholders, and probably useful ones at that. They are nontechnical and open to interpretation, a looseness of definition that buys some time. This allows us—whether teacher, administrator, researcher, or parent—to explore and evaluate some options. A few years from now I suspect other terms will become more functional—"portfolio" is one such word, "exhibition" another.

Interest in assessment methods that are closer to classroom practice is growing. This interest in performance measures and other kinds of open-ended, more naturalistic approaches to assessment is, I believe, positive. But there is not, to my knowledge, a consensus about what a new generation of assessment strategies and instruments will specifically look like. We will surely see major changes in educational assessment during the coming decade, but such change will take many forms, many directions, and evolve out of considerable trial and error.

Some Definitions

Given this context, I would like to draw attention to the language of assessment and educational evaluation. I am not usually one to spend time defining terms; however, there are occasions when it is important to take stock of language, to think about meanings we may ascribe to some critical terms. In doing this, my intention is not to offer operational or penultimate definitions, but to highlight distinctions to serve as a framework for discussions.

Assessment vs. Testing

The Encyclopedia of Educational Evaluation (Anderson et al. 1975) defines assessment as a process for gathering information to meet a variety of evaluation needs. As a process, assessment is built around multiple indicators and sources of evidence, and in this sense is distinguished from testing.

> Assessment, as opposed to simple one-dimensional measurement, is frequently described as multitrait-multimethod; that is, it focuses upon a number of variables judged to be important and utilizes a number of techniques to assay them. . . . Its techniques may also be multisource. . . and/or multijudge (p. 27).

Tests, questionnaires, interviews, ratings, unobtrusive measures, are all identified as techniques serving assessment. This definition reminds us that an assessment plan or program presumes some breadth and variety of strategies and procedures. In such a view, tests may contribute to the program, but they should not define it.

Figure 2.1 represents the scope of assessment activities as they might apply to elementary education. Such a schema, or something like it, is necessary to maintain perspective as we work on particular instruments or methodological issues.

The framework says, in effect, that a program of assessment in a school or district should be based on multiple methods, representing three quite different strands of evidence. For convenience, I have grouped various methods into three major categories of equal weight in formulating or evaluating assessment practices.

FIGURE 2.1
Assessment Program; Lines of Evidence

Observations	Performance samples	Tests or test-like
Student behaviors	Work products	procedures
(Interviews)	Artifacts	

Observation, the first source of evidence, refers to the sort of information that teachers note in everyday work with children; that is, cues in children's language and behavior that signal their interests, their thinking, their relationships. This category includes too the children's own observations and ideas about their works.

Undoubtedly, this is potentially the richest source of information, yet most elusive to recording. Rating forms, narrative descriptions, checklists, logs, and anecdotes have mixed results. The best formats for maintaining observational records are those that teachers themselves have had a hand in shaping. One person's favorite rating sheet is another's income tax form.

Performance samples are the tangible documents, or artifacts, that carry the stamp of children's accomplishments—their writing, reading, drawing, computations, constructions. In the case of literacy assessment, we have given particular attention to samples of spelling (invented), writing, drawing, dictation, and to running records of oral reading performance.

Tests refers to the full range of devices—from commercial instruments to teachers' own techniques—for checking up on student learning. In the case of reading assessment, this category might include informal reading inventories, end-of-unit tasks, and teachers' quizzes.

With this or a similar schema as a framework, a number of districts are cutting back on standardized testing, particularly in the early grades, while attempting to elevate the role of teachers' observations and samples of student performance. Few educators contest the idea that evaluation of children's progress in reading and writing should be broadly based—"multitrait-multimethod," to invoke the Encyclopedia's language. Yet, until recently, the lion's share of assessment in many districts has been consumed by testing, the mode of assessment that is the weakest and most ambiguous in what it reveals about children's strengths and capacities. The schema underscores the importance of turning to other, more direct indicators of learning.

A framework embodying multiple methods creates some space for undertaking developmental work on observational strategies or on portfolio approaches to performance. Such space is essential. If these other methods and approaches are seen as alternative forms of testing—instead of optional assessment strategies in their own right—then expectations derived from the traditions of testing are prematurely placed on new forms of instruments. These expectations may or may not be appropriate. The matter of score reliability, for example, is of great consequence for traditional achievement-testing practices that entail one-shot administration of high-stakes instruments. But it's not so important when procedures call for observations of a child across many settings, not just one; and it's not so critical in a program of assessment that calls for sampling pupil work at intervals over time.

A framework that highlights multiple strands of evidence buys time for developing and evaluating options, allowing various approaches to get off the drawing boards. Politically, it also means that you don't have to ask people to discontinue testing in all its forms; rather, you're asking for serious attention to a different order of information. One legacy of conventional testing is the expectation that a uniform set of procedures, administered on a single occasion, can satisfy multiple and sometimes conflicting needs for information and evidence. The schema provides a framework for moving away from such instrument-dominated models.

Assessment vs. Evaluation

A second aspect of the Encyclopedia's definition directs attention to a distinction between assessment and evaluation. In its derivation, the word assess means "to sit beside," to "assist the judge." It refers to a process of collecting and organizing information or data in ways that make it possible for people—teachers, parents, students—to "judge" or evaluate.

> It therefore seems appropriate . . . to limit the term assessment to the process of gathering the data and fashioning them into an interpretable form; judgments can then be made. . . . Assessment, then, as we define it, precedes the final decision-making stage in evaluation (Anderson et al. 1975, p. 27).

In an assessment program, teachers participate in a common plan of data collection and review, which might be called a plan for documentation (Chittenden and Courtney 1989). Guidelines are followed so that the data are shareable, public, and open to examination.

But the valuative judgments concerning the implications of those data—whether the judgments pertain to the progress of a child or the quality of a program—are necessarily more complex and open to debate and discussion.

Assessment data of any kind are but indicators of learning. (Webster's dictionary points out that assessment involves *estimating*, not measuring, the value of. . . .) The evidence associated with such indicators should be unambiguous to the extent that parameters of its collection are understood by teachers, parents, and students. Writing samples, reading samples (e.g., running records), and recorded observations can all be obtained via ground rules and guidelines that are commonly adopted and broadly understood. The evaluation of that evidence, however, can still be open to interpretation. Different people will form somewhat different judgments concerning the implications of the data, but any ensuing debate will be grounded in shared information.

Settings for Assessment

So much for definitions. What are some recommendations stemming from school districts' current experiences?

Based on my work with ten districts, the first general recommendation I would pass on is to spend time looking closely at assessment practices and opportunities in the classroom. New directions in school or district assessment should, wherever possible, build on classroom practices while extending them in some directions.

In the course of an ordinary school day, teachers do many things to monitor and evaluate children's learning; and while teachers do not necessarily label those things as assessment, those practices should be examined and made more explicit. For example, a useful question to pose to teachers is something on the order of: What are indications to you that a child is making progress as a reader? What does the child do? Not do? When, where?

As teachers discuss these matters, you can construct a list that captures dimensions of their answers. It will become apparent that in the primary grades, at least, teachers find indicators of children's literacy learning in a *variety* of settings. One list of settings is shown in Figure 2.2. The list will vary somewhat with particular classrooms and practices, of course, but the central message will remain: Teachers of young children can observe children's responses to books and print on many sorts of occasions, not just one "diagnostic" occasion. Children's reactions at story time, for example, provide solid indication of their comprehension of narrative; their choices at quiet reading time provide many cues about interest and habits; their oral reading and comments on texts reveal much about their strategies and facilities for dealing with print.

The database for literacy assessment in elementary classrooms is potentially a broad one. And as teachers incorporate a greater variety of activities and materials into their reading program, the base can become that much more solid. It is true, sometimes, that teachers worry that they won't know "where the children are" when they shift from a single-dimensional basal program to a more variegated, literature-based approach. But these same teachers will then be in a position to know much more about the child as a reader—about her interests, choices, strategies, and skills—because the opportunities for assessment have multiplied.

FIGURE 2.2
Classroom Settings for Assessment of Reading

Story-time: teacher reads to class (responses to story line; child's comments, questions, elaborations)

Independent reading; book-time (nature of books child chooses or brings in; process of selecting; quiet or social reading)

Reading Group/Individual (oral reading strategies: discussion of text; responses to instruction; conferences)

Reading-related activities or tasks (responses to assignments or discussion focusing on word-letter properties; word games/experience charts)

Writing (journal, stories, alphabet, dictation; invented spelling)

Informal settings (use of language in play, jokes, story-telling, conversation)

Books and print as resource (use of books for projects; attention to signs, labels, names; locating information)

Source: Chittenden, E., and R. Courtney. (1989). "Classroom-Based Assessment in Early Childhood Education." In *Emerging Literacy,* edited by Strickland and Morrow. Newark, Del.: International Reading Association.

Keeping Track, Checking Up, Finding Out

A second outcome from examining classroom assessment practices has to do with the purposes of assessment more than with specific procedures. Who is assessing whom? For what reasons?

Assessment is an attitude before it is a method. And in elementary classrooms there are three quite different attitudes or stances that teachers adopt with respect to monitoring and evaluating children's learning. Although these assessment stances are largely complementary, they sometimes conflict.

Keeping Track

The first attitude or stance might be described as one of "keeping track." What activities have children been involved in? What books has a child been reading? Which children have not yet finished the activities?

Teachers devise a great many ways for making records that serve their keeping-track concerns. Informal folders and inventories such as checklists and classlists are examples; and the children themselves can contribute to the process through daily journal entries or other modes of accounting. Over the course of a year, a fairly substantial track record of activities and accomplishments may be compiled, all under the umbrella of keeping track.

Checking Up

The second attitude of classroom assessment might be termed "checking up." Elementary teachers do this in many ways, formally and informally. Essentially, teachers ask questions or observe a child's reactions to determine whether the child has learned certain things.

In its more formal mode, checking up is synonymous with testing. Someone once defined a test as any situation in which Person A asks Person B a question to which A knows the answer. Much of this sort of interrogation goes on in our schools, whether in the guise of classroom discussions or final exams. In one way or another, we continually check up on students. Do they know the correct answer? The main idea? The point of the lesson? Notice that in each case we, the adult, presume to know the answer to the question being posed. Yet if one thinks about it, this sort of question is not characteristic of normal everyday conversations and interactions. It is peculiar to the school setting.

Finding Out

The third assessment attitude or stance is, I believe, the most interesting and probably the most critical to successful teaching. This might be termed an attitude or purpose of "finding out."

Here, the teacher's purpose is one of inquiry, of figuring out what's going on. What did the child mean? What do you suppose the children got from that story? (Versus did they get the main idea?) In this stance, teachers may again be asking questions but clearly not with the intent of checking up—an intent that is quickly communicated to children. In this case, Person A does not know the answer.

Inquiry is going on when a kindergarten teacher encourages children to talk about some of the things they noticed on a trip. There is no right answer. Or when an elementary teacher introduces a science activity by seeking evidence of the children's prior knowledge and interest: "What questions do you have about the caterpillars? Have you ever seen something like them before? Where?"

The find-out stance is fundamental to the success of the sort of decentralized and process-oriented curriculums now being advocated in many places. These curriculum statements call for instruction that is responsive to the needs, interests, and resources of the children in the classroom—particular children in particular classrooms from particular communities. This is not a canned curriculum to be implemented in standard fashion; it is instead a framework for responsive teaching.

The curriculum framework sets forth general purposes but presumes that each classroom will differ in the detail of the realization of those larger goals. Assessment-as-inquiry, as finding out, is therefore at the heart of instruction, whether such instruction goes by the name of whole language or hands-on science. Finally, to complete the picture, is a fourth stance, that of "summing up" (Engel 1990), which explicitly addresses the needs of accountability through reporting to parents, districts, and students. The effort here is aimed at organizing information in ways that are meaningful beyond the classroom door.

* * *

The development of assessment options is not just a technical matter of instrument design. Instead, to implement appropriate, practices, we need to reconsider the overall plan and purposes of educational evaluation as well as specific procedures. What sorts of information do we really need? How often? To what end? And what do students, teachers, and parents actually learn from assessment efforts?

For such reasons, new programs for documenting children's learning—as they are being developed in a number of school systems—differ from conventional assessment practices along several dimensions. For instance:

New assessment practices:	*Conventional practices:*
• Are ongoing, cumulative	• Are annual
• Use open-ended formats	• Are multiple-choice
• Draw upon a variety of settings	• Are based on a single setting
• Are theory-referenced	• Are norm-referenced
• Are teacher-mediated	• Are teacher-proof

Without adequate attention to the design and function of assessment programs, there is little reason to expect that new kinds of instruments, as embodied in portfolios, performance tasks, or other formats, will prove worth the effort.

We need to give three quite different lines of evidence proportionate attention when we develop options for documenting children's learning. We also need to differentiate between assessment activities and the evaluations they serve. That is, ground rules for collecting and organizing information can be designed without insisting on standardization of judgment. Finally, the point of departure in constructing more sensitive assessment strategies should be the examination of classroom practice. If the methods or strategies don't make sense at this very local level, there is little reason to push toward wider implementation.

References

Anderson, S., S. Ball, R. Murphy, and associates. (1975). *Encyclopedia of Educational Evaluation*. San Francisco: Jossey-Bass.

Chittenden, E., and R. Courtney. (1989). "Assessment of Young Children's Reading: Documentation as an Alternative to Testing." In *Emerging Literacy*, edited by Strickland and Morrow. Newark, Del.: International Reading Association.

Engel, B. "An Approach to Assessment in Early Literacy." (1990). In *Achievement Testing in the Early Grades: The Games Adults Play*, edited by Kamii. Washington, D.C.: National Association for the Education of Young Children.

3

Building a School Culture of High Standards: A Teacher's Perspective

Ron Berger

As a 6th grade teacher, my concept of a culture of high standards includes high standards for kindness and cooperation as well as for academic work. Just as I emphasize that careful quality in work is more important than fast production, I pay careful attention to treating all students fairly and thoughtfully, rather than stressing efficiency and speed in school logistics. For example, "simple" classroom decisions, such as which students should make a presentation or attend a limited event, often take a long time because my students and I discuss such issues carefully, considering the feelings of all. In my class, we avoid events and honors that are exclusionary or individualistic, displays of the "best" work or awards for the "best" students or athletes. Rather, we favor whole-class, whole-student pride. When visitors to my classroom are impressed with student work, it is often due not to specific outstanding examples but rather to the absence of careless work, the uniform commitment to quality. This is a testament to the degree of cultural pride and peer support in the classroom.

Much of what goes on in a traditional classroom, in terms of structure of work, assessment, and models of relationships, serves to undermine and negate such a supportive class culture. The model of classroom roles and assessment in my school, therefore, differs from traditional conceptions. Although the school itself is fairly typical—it's a regular public elementary school in a rural New England town—its approach to learning is not. Student work is not centered on textbooks and worksheets, but rather on individual and group projects that are rich in skills and content. Students "publish" books, draft maps, and make blueprints. They prepare research papers, build scale models, manage long-term experiments, and share these projects through displays and presentations for the school and town. Every student, whether mainstream or marginal, is an equal member of each classroom's "project workshop." All students are expected to do the highest quality work—and are supported in their efforts. Students with learning or other disabilities remain in the classroom as part of the working team. Students are encouraged and taught to help each other as editors, critics, collaborators, and tutors.

Every final draft, project, or presentation emerging from a classroom workshop reflects on the whole class. Each, therefore, must show great care and effort and must be accurate, powerful, and elegant. Students, as well as teachers, enforce these standards. Like an athletic team, everyone's performance affects the group; helping each other helps everyone.

The focus on team effort, on whole-class, whole-school commitment to quality, has profound effects on the success of individuals. Because of this, people in town who were initially suspicious and critical of the school's untraditional approach have become strong school supporters. The excitement, accomplishments, and thoughtfulness of students have won over the hearts of a rural and fairly conservative town. There is a great deal of pride in the school.

Modeling Behavior

I begin the year doing a lot of modeling. Many teachers say they model behavior for students, and many do. Quite often, however, teacher modeling is superficial. To really model, one must do the same things that students do, so that modeling is real and fair. In my classes, I try to actually work on those tasks that I require of students—project work, math problems, cleaning the sink, caring for classroom animals, giving and accepting criticism and support—in front of students. The most important thing I model for students is taking risks: taking the risk of sharing my real feelings with them, of trying things in front of them that I'm not good at, of admitting my mistakes and confusions, and of accepting and inviting constructive criticism from students. I share my worries and mistakes in directing the class and in planning lessons. I share the rough drafts of project work I'm pursuing along with them, criticize my own work, and invite suggestions and opinions. I don't allow students to be rude or derisive to me—or to other students; but I try to welcome suggestions concerning how I could improve and grow. If I'm

trying to build an environment of risk-taking and learning, I need to be
the head risk taker and head learner.

Deemphasizing Grades

Assessment must be planned so that it does not suppress risk-taking
and cooperation, nor discourage learners who are struggling. For this
reason, very little work in my classroom and school is given formal
grades, and report cards are narrative. Letter grades are not used at all;
percentages or points are used occasionally, but only in test situations.
This policy creates a lot of work for teachers and frustrates some parents
who yearn for the finality of grades. (Most parents, however, are pleased
with the careful narrative reports and the parent conferences in which
student projects and progress are shared and discussed.) This lack of
constant grading creates a school in which there are no "C" or "D"
students who have given up on caring and trying, there is no established
hierarchy of "smart kids" and "dumb kids," and students and teachers are
concerned with the quality of work rather than letter grades. Student
projects are never graded: the wonderful sense of shared group success
and achievement would be deflated and soured by rewarding some
students and discouraging others. This does not mean there is a lack of
assessment of project work. Students receive copious feedback at all
points during the creation of the project from teachers and from peers,
and they are well aware of their project's strengths and weaknesses. With
nongraded assessment, however, even the least talented of students,
having done a personally exemplary job, can feel pride in the whole-class
presentation of successful work, rather than feel shame in receiving a
poor grade.

Some critics of giving formal letter grades contend that although
letter grades are motivating to "A" students, who get all the positive
reinforcement, grades persuade "C" or "D" students that their ability is
small and that it's a waste of time to try too hard. I would go further: I
think grades are destructive even for "A" students. In these students, an
emphasis on letter grades encourages a narrow-minded pursuit of
conservative and proven strategies to please. Imagine if we, as adults,
were given letter grades on all of the functions we undertake in our jobs.
Think of how tense and defensive this would make us, and how quickly
we would adjust our behavior to perform in constricted, uncreative
patterns that would protect against bad grades. Finally, giving grades to
the class, particularly on the "fair" system of a curve, gives an unequivocal

message, and in my view an insane one, that the worse your classmates do, the better for you.

Practicing Test Taking

Some teachers give a lot of tests. I do not. Except in math, they are a relatively minor part of assessment for me. When students leave school, they are judged for the rest of their lives by the quality of work they produce and the quality of personal skills they possess, not by their ability to take tests. If I want students to put their full hearts into becoming better workers and more thoughtful people, then it is their work and effort that must be the basis of assessment.

I give tests occasionally, but with a different purpose: I think the skills of studying for tests and taking tests are essential skills for students to have if they hope to succeed in today's schools. I present tests to students in exactly this way: test preparation and test taking are important skills, and we'll all work together as a group to get better at them. I allow students to take the same test, or a clone, over and over again until they feel they have succeeded. I share every test-taking tip I know; and I encourage students to work together, tutor each other, and share strategies. We celebrate anyone's growth on tests, as well as our collective growth as a class. Testing skills are not presented as equivalent to talent or personal worth, simply as another important skill.

Assessing by Critiques

In my classroom, most assessment takes the form of conferences and critique—either formal or, almost unconsciously, informal— throughout the day. Assessment is most often a process of shepherding growth, rather than deriving a final grade or level. It is the transition from formal critique to ongoing informal critique that signifies to me the real adoption of the culture of high standards.

Formal Critique

Initially, I present and model how to critique in whole-class sessions. Some of my students and I all bring early drafts of work and share them with the group for appraisal. The people sharing their work begin by explaining what they are trying to achieve with the piece, and students offer opinions of what in the piece seems to be succeeding in this intent, and what may be detracting. This structure means that the comments are not in the form of "it's good" (understood as "you're good"), or "it's bad (you're bad)," but rather, "it's working for what you want in these ways, but not in these ways."

A goal is to involve students in a method of critique that is precise and constructive, unlike the all-too-common type of classroom critique that is limited to variations of "I like your story; it's good." Recently, I learned about a useful metaphor for describing critique to students: it is like surgery—opening up a piece, taking it apart, to discover what is working and what is not. The surgical tools we have are words; the more deep and precise our vocabulary in the field, the more precise we can be at seeing and understanding the piece we are analyzing. If our vocabulary is limited to "good" and "bad," our surgical kit has only one tool; it's like trying to do surgery with a cleaver—you can't see or separate much of anything. If a critique of a student's story entails talk of dialogue, setting, scene description, plot tension, foreshadowing, irony, character development, symbolism, metaphor, humor, and other components of fiction, there is a possibility that the workings of this story can be revealed, understood, and improved. Critique of a science experiment is severely limited if students can't speak in terms of hypothesis, methods, control, variables, data observation, validity of results, significance of results. These are more than words, they are concepts; they are lenses that allow us to see the work.

The vocabulary that forms the basis of critique sessions is basically the working vocabulary of practitioners in that field. For this reason, I like to have "experts," professionals or craftspeople in a field, visit the class and teach us this vocabulary. In some fields I may have a good grasp of much of the vocabulary; in others I am as ignorant as the students. Either way, expert visitors allow students and teacher to learn together. For example, during an interdisciplinary study of architecture in 1991, my class hosted five architects at various times. The architects gave presentations and critiqued student work. Without the concepts and technical language we learned from these practitioners, we never could have viewed and critiqued our own design efforts capably. We had similar experiences with other visitors: a landform geologist, an Egyptologist, a graphic artist, a children's book author, and a university women's soccer team. To highlight one example, when students began to model the language of the soccer players and the strategies they defined, both the style of play in student games and the level of postgame analysis changed dramatically. Students now had precise terms to describe particular passes, defenses, shots, and movements; and they revelled in this new vocabulary on the field, shouting directions and ideas while playing, even seeing options that before wouldn't have occurred to them.

Spontaneous Critique

Just as important as formal critique sessions are spontaneous ones. Quite often, the class just jumps into an analysis of something and ignores other work for a moment. It may be an informal critique of the cover of a book we've just gotten, a school assembly we just attended, a political event, a television show, or a recess soccer game. At first, some students view this as a "trick" that succeeds in distracting me, as teacher, from "real work." They soon come to see that I am not distracted at all: that I value this critique as real work and am often pleased to take a short break to attend to it—and, in fact, I often initiate it. Because students see that I'm serious about critique, they take it seriously. Perhaps serious is not the best description; these sessions are fun and animated, but they are as much a part of the classroom as "real work."

Encouraging Student Appraisals

The most important assessment of all takes place on a smaller and even more informal level. When educators talk of assessment, they generally think in terms of documented assessment systems. A completely different level of assessment takes place in the individual student, who is constantly assessing her own work, deciding what is right and wrong, what fits and what does not, what is a "good enough" job. This self-appraisal is the ultimate locus of all standards.

Just beyond this level is the assessment of peers. Recently some schools have begun to use formal modes of peer assessment, either in peer conferences or group critiques; but most peer assessment is not a formal process. It takes place on a deeper level, one that isn't usually articulated. Students look around them as they work; they watch the quality of what their friends turn in, what others can "get away with" for standards, what is displayed, and what is praised or valued in the peer group. In this way they determine what is appropriate and acceptable behavior and work. Quite often students in traditional classrooms consciously lower their standards to blend in more comfortably with peer notions of proper behavior or attitude for a boy or girl their age.

Infusing these two informal levels of assessment—self-appraisal and peer appraisal—with a commitment to high standards is the ultimate goal of all the larger, formal structures in the class. When high standards reach into those levels, then I know the culture has taken hold. As the year goes on, there is less and less need for planned, formal critique, because students practice ongoing assessment throughout the day. Students work on projects at tables or desks; they constantly seek help, advice, and criticism from each other—and they are not shy about giving it. A student walking by a table where a peer is working on a project will often stop to analyze the piece, ask questions about choices made, compliment strengths, and give opinions and advice concerning what he feels is "working" in the piece.

Student analysis of personal or peer work can get quite technical and obsessive; I welcome this. Outside of school, students often engage in long-term interests that they pursue passionately: collecting baseball cards; practicing video games; arranging dollhouses; building models; and structuring fantasy play with dolls, action figures, or other toys. These are often ongoing projects that are obsessive and technical in detail and care. It is this type of intensity that I try to harness and draw into the classroom through project work. The excitement and precision students bring to building and critiquing projects is almost identical to what they put into making miniature dollhouse furniture at home, or arranging their baseball cards in sets of notebooks and making elaborate inventory and price lists. The intensity and focus of peer discussion and appraisal of work in the classroom is what fuels the quality of this work and what defines the culture of standards. In this environment, students often turn to each other, rather than the teacher, for feedback, assistance, and suggestions; the explicit locus of assessment and approval shifts away from the teacher and toward peers.

Developing Portfolios

Students in my classroom keep four different portfolios of their work: a reading portfolio, a writing portfolio, a technical design portfolio, and a large portfolio for artwork and large project work. If teachers, parents, visitors, peers, or students themselves need to view or appraise their work, they have a wealth of rough draft and final draft material to draw upon.

These days I carry around a portfolio of student projects: science projects, mathematics projects, student literature, videotapes of plays, and many projects that cross disciplines and can't be easily placed in any one. When I start to feel that my descriptions of this approach to learning are mostly hot air, a hype, another new gimmick in the age-old and rarely improved business of teaching, I have something real and tangible to renew my faith, to share with others. These projects and the accomplishments they represent for students are evidence for me that many aspects of the "good old days" can be substantially improved upon.

Student work in my classroom is like nothing I did when I was a child in public school. Even in high school, I was rarely allowed the opportunity to design and direct an important long-range project. Almost nothing I created during 13 years of schooling was an artifact that I treasured, that I kept and admired over the years. In contrast, the work I carry around today is on loan from students. Many students were unwilling to part with their projects, even for a year, so I could use them in workshops; those who agreed were sometimes nervous about it. Two students have contacted me this year to confirm that their projects were still all right, and one asked to borrow his back for a presentation in his science class. As a child, I was a student whom teachers would have categorized as highly motivated and perfectionist; yet little I created had lasting value for me. Few school experiences had the emotional involvement that projects, performances, presentations, and trips do for my students today. And I was an example of classroom success, a model student, while Jimmy P. and the rest of the back row had been given up as lost causes since 2nd grade.

My teachers in elementary school often instructed us to "try to do your best." This isn't a bad motto; I'd use it with my class today, and most schools would embrace it without a thought. There's a big step, though, between teachers' saying this to students, and students' actually doing it. Not too many schools seriously look at what aspects of their structure and culture support and compel students to do their best, to act their best, and what aspects undermine this spirit. Rather than simply search for individual teachers or principals who they hope can demand high standards, I feel that school communities should discover how they can create a spirit of high standards, a school culture of high standards.

4

Tapping Teachers' Knowledge

David Carroll and Patricia Carini

Because teachers spend so much time with children, they have a unique and valuable vantage point for gaining knowledge about their ways of thinking and learning. They can note subtle patterns and continuities that persons outside the classroom, however knowledgeable they may be about children, simply cannot observe. The knowledge that teachers form in this way is relevant to the classroom—because it arises there.

Some educators think only a few truly gifted and dedicated teachers can obtain this kind of knowledge. Their disparaging attitude often leads to a lowest-common-denominator approach to school organization and accountability. In the worst cases, policymakers mandate an overly specific curriculum, and assessment is used as much for checking up on teachers as for monitoring student progress.

Assessment usually takes the form of standardized tests that reduce children's efforts as learners to numbers that indicate how many questions each child answered correctly on the day the test was given. These snapshot assessments miss fundamental qualities of human effort and possibility: subtleties of thought, patterns of effort over time, areas of interest or wonder that promote further learning, emerging self-awareness. If we rely on standardized tests to assess student learning, we come away with a distorted view of learning. Teachers can overcome that distortion, however, by using their knowledge of students to conduct their own assessments.

A Real-Life Example

The story of Sid (a pseudonym) illustrates a way of assessing children's school experiences that offers a reliable means for tapping teachers' knowledge and ensuring its continued development.

Sid is a tall, lanky nine-year-old with an insistent voice and awkward movements. When he first entered Prospect School* as an eight-year-old, he frequently irritated his fellow students. He bumped into them, jarred them with loud noises, or disturbed their work. His apparent obliviousness to his own actions and his nervousness at being called to account for them were puzzling to his teacher, Jessica Howard. Because Sid reacted to conflict with panic and denial, Howard had to mediate to secure for him a degree of acceptance from his classmates. Her efforts to encourage greater self-consciousness and responsibility met with meager success.

When an idea caught his interest, though, Sid's face would light up with wonder. His full attention was captured by anything puzzling or mysterious, a problem requiring analysis, or connections to be found among an array of elements. An avid but careless reader, he was also full of information.

Following school custom, Sid began his second year at Prospect School in the same multi-age class he had studied with the previous year. Howard had worked with Sid for over a year now, keeping the usual narrative records of his activity choices and interests, the ease or difficulty of his social relations, and snippets of interesting conversations or remarks.

She noticed that Sid seemed frustrated by not being able to express in words certain things he thought and felt. Yet Sid enjoyed reading aloud—expressing feeling in a controlled context before an audience. Howard decided to pursue this observation by presenting Sid to her colleagues at Prospect School's weekly "Descriptive Review of the Child" meeting.

The "Descriptive Review of the Child" Meeting

The Descriptive Review was developed at Prospect to give teachers and other educators the opportunity to gain a deeper collective understanding of children and childhood by focusing on a teacher's description of a particular child. The purpose of the review is not to change the child, not to explain certain behaviors, not to "fix up" perceived problems, but to help the presenting teacher become more

---

*Prospect School is a private, nonprofit school in North Bennington, Vermont, serving approximately 60 children, aged 4½ to 14, from diverse backgrounds. The school assigns children to multi-age groups, allowing them to remain for up to three years with the same teacher and the same classmates.

attuned to the child's strengths and possibilities as a person and a learner. Any specific concerns about the child are discussed within that broader understanding.

The typical procedure for the Descriptive Review calls for a chair whose responsibility is to conduct the meeting in such a manner that the integrity and dignity of the child, the presenting teacher, and the family are protected. Toward this end, the meeting follows agreed upon procedures and observes ordinary customs of courtesy. More important, it is guided by commitments to portraying the child in as full and complete a way as possible and with particular attention to his or her strengths.

When Howard described her concern about Sid's struggles to express himself, she did not expect her colleagues to help her find a five-step plan to teach him to be expressive. Instead, she sought to expand her own perspectives and understandings, knowing that a fuller picture of Sid and a better grasp of his strengths would help her find ways to support him in the classroom.

Howard began by stating her "presenting question" or concern. She described Sid as expressive and lively when talking about ideas and information, but uncomfortable in situations calling for a statement of value or feeling, such as when settling a social conflict. Sid's puzzlement, his flat emotional tone, and his urgency to conclude such situations hindered conversation or stopped it altogether. Howard said she believed Sid found these occasions as frustrating and unsatisfactory as she and his classmates did.

She gave her colleagues a full description of Sid, according to the customary headings of the Descriptive Review process: his physical presence and gestures, temperament and disposition, relationships with others, interests and activities, and formal learning. She had prepared the description by reviewing the narrative records she had kept over the previous months.

Her presentation included a listing of Sid's preferred activities in the classroom: drawing and storytelling with others, building marble chutes and mazes with blocks, making small plasticene (a kind of clay) figures for dramatic play, cooking, and intricate construction activities. She said that Sid was also interested in formal dramatic productions; when performing, he was animated and graceful, displaying a real talent for clever improvisation and embellishment. His sense of timing, pace, expression, and imagery were right on the mark from the first rehearsal, suggesting an ability to grasp with remarkable ease and quickness the tone of the play and an overall idea of the plot.

Turning to formal learning, Howard described Sid's progress in reading, writing, math, social studies, and science. She emphasized his breadth of understanding and inattention to detail in all areas. The latter was most noticeable in his writing, which she characterized as fluent and expressive but marred by extremely sloppy handwriting.

Sid's breadth of understanding was especially well illustrated by his work in math. Howard explained that he often created his own processes for solving certain kinds of computation problems. For example, when asked to add 27 and 8, Sid replied, "Well, add 3 to the 7, that makes 30 . . . so, 35." His approaches usually left implicit such steps as the compensation of subtracting 3 from 8 in this example. These details often tripped Sid up unless Howard, recognizing his unconventional procedure, explained how the approach he had invented fit into the number system. Sid took great pleasure in these explanations and put them to good use.

In reading, Howard said that Sid preferred a book like *The Hobbit* that offered him a whole world to explore and a landscape made for heroic adventure. Sid's mental travels through that landscape were rapid because his attention was focused on the action. Covering the terrain in giant steps, he often overlooked key details while absorbed in the unfolding drama. Here, too, he was grateful for adult support in sorting out the story.

Discussion and Recommendations

When Howard had finished her presentation, the chair summarized what had been said: Sid was described as a large-scale, intuitive thinker—he saw the big picture, even if he faltered when asked to clarify it for someone else. The chair called attention to the inward, self-referential quality of Sid's thinking, illustrated in the working out of his own mathematical procedures, and speculated that Sid's immediate "feel" for the right dramatic gesture suggested a dimension of his thinking and self that was especially animated, vivid, and emotionally charged.

In the discussion following the presentation, the group suggested a link between the idea of Sid's inhabiting a relatively closed inner world and the distance he must travel when expected to communicate with others. Also, the group noted that absorption in his own point of view, however dramatic or original, did not leave much room for others' points of view; nor did it predispose him to hear the vocabulary and discourse for negotiating social conflicts.

In support of these conjectures, the others observed that Sid effectively placed Howard in the position of tracing the perimeters of social situations for him, bringing definition to his own big picture, and allowing him to think and act with confidence. They also compared the value-laden conflicts that left Sid tongue-tied with the equally emotive, but more bounded and controllable, realms of literature and drama. The latter, because they are controllable, allowed Sid safe access to a wealth of strong feeling. Social tensions among peers, however, offered none of the security of foretelling and control.

The group then recommended courses of action and a focus for future observations to continue to support Sid in the classroom. Several supports that Howard was already providing were affirmed, sometimes with suggestions for enhancing or expanding them. For example, because Howard's drawing of the boundaries of social situations was clearly helpful to Sid, the group suggested that this approach be used more intentionally and consistently. They also suggested using the vocabulary of "mapping out" to connect with Sid's own talents for internally mapping a large picture or context.

Expanding on the ideas of mapping out and seeing the big picture, they suggested that mapping itself was an apt metaphor for one of Sid's preferred ways of knowing and learning; therefore, offering mapping as an activity seemed promising. They noted that mapping as a way of forming knowledge was applicable across the disciplines: timelines in history, classifications and categories in science, patterns in mathematics, and so on.

To expand the repertoire of the classroom dramatic activities so useful to Sid, the group recommended choral reading, radio plays based on books, and "air bands," a form of lip syncing to the accompaniment of popular music. To increase Sid's access to expressed but bounded feeling and imagery, the teachers recommended using more music and poetry.

Finally, the teachers agreed that Sid seemed to be on the right track; he just needed more time and more occasions to find and make his own connections. A classroom offering him daily social contact with other youngsters, with adults available to mediate that interchange, was in and of itself an invaluable support to him.

Report to Parents

Howard's end-of-year report to Sid and his parents included comments that reflected the insights gained in the descriptive review:

> Sid's term has been predictably full and productive for him. He continues to invest in his projects with energy and enthusiasm. His relationship to the group has stabilized, though Sid still has ups and downs. . . . Sid himself is less self-excusing about difficult incidents . . . more articulate and outspoken about how he is feeling; and certainly more aware after the fact of how he contributed to the difficulties. On the whole, Sid has a good, steady, visible place in the group and a variety of associates to choose from for his activities. . . .

Why It Works

The descriptive review process works because it offers a way to make the knowledge teachers obtain from daily work in classrooms public and accessible to supportive colleagues. It offers an opportunity to deepen thought and refine language about children and classrooms; it works against easy labels and facile prescriptions.

It works also because it embeds particular urgent concerns or specific events in a broader and longer-term account of the child. It reveals characteristic patterns in interests, choices, ways of perceiving and constructing order, and modes of thinking and learning. In Sid's case, it revealed a pattern of strength in large-scale thought and intuitive vision when what was initially most prominent was social awkwardness and gaps in language. Recognizing this pattern enabled his teacher to contemplate alternative approaches that supported Sid's overall education while allowing him to draw on his strengths.

A thorough descriptive review session normally requires one and a half to two hours. Even though the group cannot usually review every child in a class, looking closely at just a few children can enrich a teacher's understanding of the whole class. In discussing one child's particular qualities, teachers are often reminded of similar or contrasting qualities of other children. Moreover, gaining new insights about one child alerts teachers to the power of their own knowledge and makes them feel confident that they can use it to address other circumstances as well.

Finally, this assessment method offers an opportunity to reconceive the relationship between schools and parents. It sets the tone for ongoing collaboration between home and school based on a mutual effort to identify and support children's interests and strengths.

Teachers' narrative records, reports to parents, and the descriptive review itself keep assessment close to the classroom and preserve the knowledge it yields for those most able to benefit from it—children, parents, and other educators.

5

Authentic Assessment: Beyond the Buzzword and Into the Classroom

Rieneke Zessoules and Howard Gardner

The scene is a familiar one: neatly aligned rows of desks, sharp, yellow No. 2 pencils in the hands of restless students waiting for the seal to be broken on stacks of freshly printed testing booklets. Inevitability permeates the room, as exam booklets are passed, one by one, through the rows. There is a strain of resignation to the teacher's voice as she reads from the scripted text: "Clean off your desk. Fill in the circles completely. Press down firmly so the computer can read your answer sheets. OK, now begin; you have 20 minutes to complete this portion of the test. Answer the questions to the best of your ability." The sound of scratching pencils fills the room as students work rapidly to complete analogies, recognize vocabulary words, and make simple calculations. With each question, students pause to select and carefully blacken the circles that punctuate the page. The work is serious, and the stakes are high. For better or worse, these students and this teacher are part of a drama in which all American education participates.

Little is exotic about this scenario. Standardized testing is recognized widely as the instrument, if not the model, for measuring student learning across the country. Standardized tests exert a powerful

Authors' note: The work described here was supported by grants from the Grant Foundation, the Lilly Endowment, the Markle Foundation, and the Spencer Foundation. Our examples were taken from the work of Arts Propel, a five-year collaborative project with the Pittsburgh Public Schools and the Educational Testing Service, supported by the Rockefeller Foundation. We are indebted to the students, teachers, and administrators in Pittsburgh, Boston, Indianapolis, and Cambridge for their work and efforts in the practice of authentic assessment. Our discussions included interviews with Jerry Halpern, Langley High School, Pittsburgh, Pennsylvania, and Barbara Ehrlich, Cambridge Rindge and Latin High School, Cambridge, Massachusetts. In addition, we would like to thank Dennie Wolf and John Mester for their insights and ongoing conversations about this work.

hold on classroom experience. The National Center for Fair and Open Testing estimates that each American child takes as many as three such standardized tests every school year (Neill and Medina 1989). These tests determine which classes students will take, which schools they can attend, and even which level of academic potential they are expected to achieve. Standardized tests influence, where they do not dictate, decisions about institutional goals, teacher performance, and program funding. Not surprisingly, these measures drive the curriculums in our schools and dominate instruction in the classroom (Gifford 1990). But the power of assessment to affect and shape teaching and learning in the classroom needs to be examined.

In our view, American society has embraced standardized testing to an excessive degree. Indeed, these measures form an underlying "testing" culture throughout schools and school systems, one that sustains an equally standardized approach to learning and evaluation. Despite the universality of this testing culture, there is reason to question its legitimacy. Observe a skilled teacher as she assesses students' work: looking for more than just information possessed, she depends not on discrete instances but entire performances, sampled frequently over time in the classroom. The teacher monitors students' capacities for being thoughtful, creative, curious, and self-directed. She watches for students to make use of the skills they have learned in a variety of contexts— making judgments, drawing connections to their own world and experiences, applying new understandings in thoughtful and meaningful ways.

In this teacher's classroom, you are likely to see tables filled with lab equipment, pieces of student work in various stages of completion, or desks pushed aside to make room for group activities and discussion. Students are likely to be moving around the room questioning, experimenting, talking, debating, and looking. They may work on a project for hours, days, or weeks—designing experiments, conducting interviews, crafting oral history projects, deriving equations and testing theories, or writing and revising multiple drafts of a short story. In each of these cases, students are engaged in a variety of activities, constructing strategies for demonstrating their understanding. Through these activities, students show that they know how to develop ideas; pose questions; experiment with new possibilities; and revise, refine, and present their work.

Observations and performance reviews of this kind have begun to exert a powerful influence on new models of assessment. In the wake of the concerns about standardized measures, individual teachers, districts, and states are developing new kinds of testing measures based on entire performances. Currently taking the form chiefly of portfolios and performance-based tasks, these measures are often referred to as *authentic assessment;* and they are designed to present a broader, more genuine picture of student learning. While still experimental, these measures have intrigued a growing number of concerned educators across the country. Authentic assessment is fast becoming the buzzword of hope among educators who value more expansive descriptions of learning. Many schools are suddenly looking to have "it" in their classrooms.

One example of an authentic assessment is the New York State Grade 4 Manipulative Skills Test. This hands-on science test transforms the classroom into a science lab with equipment distributed across the rows and columns of desks. Homemade balances, electrical batteries and light bulbs, trays filled with objects and instruments are placed about the room to form various stations: measuring objects, experimenting with water, grouping objects, testing electricity, and investigating hidden properties of "mystery objects." Every student has a turn at each station. In each case, students are given time to experiment with the appropriate instruments to study and solve a series of questions. For example, at the "measuring station," rather than filling in the names of all the parts on a diagram of a balance, students must demonstrate that they know how to make measurements. Using pennies, rulers, and thermometers to measure and compare various objects, students show that they understand something about the system of weights and measures and that they can apply that knowledge in a variety of contexts. At the "water station," students must use their observational skills to first study and then predict what will happen when they immerse various objects in water. Likewise, at each of the remaining stations, students use and manipulate lab equipment to study nature and solve scientific problems. Whereas standardized tests require students to demonstrate possession of knowledge and recollection of basic, scientific facts, these students in New York are required to demonstrate a deeper understanding of scientific principles (Mitchell 1989).

But assessment cannot be only a matter of building fancier, better, or truer tests. As should be evident, such rich modes of assessment cannot be activated in a vacuum. Just as standardized tests have produced a testing culture, educators interested in reform must recognize and examine the need for a classroom culture that will sustain the values, merits and practices of more authentic forms of assessment. If one is going to ask students to complete analogies, recall information, or perform basic calculations under time pressure, one needs a curriculum in which students have regular opportunities to form analogies, memorize facts, and manipulate equations with speed. By the same token, if one is going to ask students to grasp scientific principles, compose a melody, or write compelling dialogues, then one needs a curriculum that gives students frequent opportunities to investigate, test, and observe nature; to compose and experiment with many melodies; and to craft, rehearse, and revise many scenes, many times. Just as standardized testing has driven curriculum and instruction in our schools, so too the implementation of new measures must influence and shape the daily life and activities in the classroom. Unless new modes of assessment reach deep into school culture, incorporating pedagogical approaches, expectations and standards of performance, and the education of students' own capacities for self-critical judgment, new forms of testing will be as discontinuous with teaching and learning as they have ever been.

Consequently, in this chapter, we draw a distinction between the singular act of testing and the complex processes of assessment. Concerned educators who want to change the scope, function, and goal of assessment practices in the schools must look beyond the simple modification of current instrumentation. We examine how a different, fuller, and more contextual form of assessment might become an integrated portion of what and how we teach our children. We begin by describing the conditions and practices that lay the foundation for an assessment culture in the classroom. We then consider the implications of adopting an assessment culture in our schools.

Many of the examples we use come from work conducted at Harvard Project Zero as part of a long-term investigation of new modes of assessment. In particular, we cite several examples from the Arts Propel project. This project grew out of the need for urban schools to monitor work and learning in areas that commonly fall outside of standardized testing—in particular, students' accomplishments and growing understandings in music, visual arts, and imaginative writing. The resulting three-way collaboration among Pittsburgh Public Schools, Educational Testing Service, and Harvard Project Zero has led specifically to the development of classroom projects and student portfolios as tools for teaching, learning, and assessment.

Laying the Foundation for Authentic Assessment Practices

Much of our work at Project Zero has centered on investigating and articulating the kind of classroom environments that both support and provoke authentic assessment practices. In our search, we have found four critical conditions for the establishment of an assessment culture in the classroom. These classroom conditions include nurturing complex understandings, developing reflective habits of mind, documenting students' evolving understandings, and making use of assessment as a moment of learning. In our view, these classrooms are, in fact, the only classrooms where students are truly being prepared for authentic assessment. In this section we investigate each of these conditions and practices through examples from a range of different classrooms.

Nurturing Complex Understandings

Assessment is typically associated with the possession of information, rather than the mastery of ongoing processes (like learning to write, revise, and take criticism or, even more radically, to integrate the results of a critique into a work). Most current forms of assessment require highly specialized, yet surprisingly superficial, kinds of knowledge. We test students for what they know rather than what they understand. Yet these kinds of skills have little or no relevance beyond school walls. Individuals outside of the classroom are rarely, if ever, asked to diagram sentences, draw a color wheel, complete an isolated analogy, or fill in missing pieces of a mathematical formula. Instead, they are expected to pursue projects over time, to collaborate and converse with others, to take responsibility for their work—provoking and engaging in reflection and revision—and to amplify their understandings and apply them in powerful ways or in new or surprising contexts. If assessment is to be a moment in an educational process rather than simply an evaluative vehicle, then it must be seen and used as an opportunity to develop complex understandings. We follow with one example of how assessment can be combined with learning and instruction to provide a powerful instance of authentic assessment through the building, nurturing, and practicing of rich understandings.

Barbara Ehrlich teaches choreography to high school dance students at Cambridge Rindge and Latin High School in Cambridge, Massachusetts. She is very clear about what she thinks her students should be able to know and do:

Choreography isn't a kind of magical thing. I really want them to know that's true—even with technique. None of this is magic; it's hard work. I always say to them, you think writing a paper is bad, you should try this! But it's more than the end-product that's the masterpiece here. After all, anybody who does this seriously and sincerely, no matter what their technique level, can create something quite lovely. The most valuable accomplishment is the process of how you got there. Number one, you wanted to communicate something that was inside of you and you didn't want to write it or paint it, you wanted to create an image in movement. Number two, you had to do it in a way that was yours—not somebody else's—not a teacher who comes and says now do this step and this step. This is about developing your own expressive language of movement. And number three, you had to work with somebody to figure this thing out. It's not like this dance happens spontaneously. There is this process that you have to work through together: moving, watching, composing, experimenting, reflecting, rehearsing, and critiquing—finding new ways to express your ideas. This is what making a dance is all about (Zessoules 1988).

Ehrlich's students are learning more than how to string together movement; they are learning to think and work as choreographers. This kind of understanding is not about sudden bursts of creative energy, or threading together interesting shapes and gestures; it is about being able to enter into a piece of work from a variety of different perspectives (Wolf 1989). For these students, the making of a dance is rich with experience and detail. Such full-bodied experiences are not created accidently. They are the result of careful layering of new and different frames of reference, at any one moment, challenging students to approach their work as maker, perceiver, and critic (Zessoules, Wolf, and Gardner 1988). It is this blending of stances that leads to the kind of thoughtfulness and understanding needed to think and work as a choreographer.

The teenagers that come to Ehrlich's class are, in their own ways, masters of movement. Their everyday lives are chock full of the silent signals of gesture, movement, and body language. But when they think of dance, they tend to think of a chain of technical moves and shapes, not an expression of an idea through the images and language of dance. Ehrlich seeks to change that. Her students are not technicians executing a series of steps, nor are they passive consumers, watching, but never experiencing, what it means to create a dance. Ehrlich wants her students to be artists and active learners: to take on the role of dancer, choreographer, and critic (Zessoules 1989).

In the beginning, Ehrlich encourages her students to use all the insights and knowledge they bring as experts in the language of gesture. Experimenting with ordinary, everyday movement, Ehrlich tells her students, "Today you are not 'movers' but 'dancers.'" And they plunge right in, composing short phrases and signatures, taking ordinary movements and abstracting and amplifying them to make them into dances. The playfulness of these exercises helps students learn about the language of dance and its relationship to everyday motion and movement. Already, they are beginning to understand the difference between ordinary and extraordinary movement.

Then Ehrlich's students enter this work from a new perspective. Through a series of group pieces directed by Ehrlich, students are thrust into performance, learning by experiencing the art of dance. During this phase, they also watch videos and live performances with rapt attention, and they watch each other, stopping to talk about what they see and think. They learn what it means to create compelling images, to play with the rhythm and balance in them, and to convey an idea through them. This is how they learn the standards of excellence and performance in dance.

As the layers of understanding accumulate, Ehrlich steps quietly out of the picture so that her students are responsible for adding the next layer of understanding: the creation of original works. Given the task of crafting their own pieces for the dance concert in May, her students are now the artists, and Ehrlich is the careful observer. By assuming the role of the choreographer, these students have entered deeply into the art and craft of making dances. They work diligently, experimenting, revising, polishing, and reworking their pieces.

Ehrlich pushes them one step further by adding the dimension of a real and critical audience for their dances. Weekly progress checks are established, in which students learn the importance of a wider audience for their work. Here they must approach their work from yet another perspective: the role of reflective critic. Every week students share their works in progress, asking for and providing feedback and helping each other plow the results back into their dances. Here they learn the importance of reflection, and they begin to see how their work affects others. This is how these young choreographers begin to understand the power of dance as a unique form of expression and communication.

In addition, students keep journals full of notes as they work together to improve their dances and prepare them for the final concert. Their reflection about this work and process will not end with the concert in May. They will spend the month of June re-creating and reviewing the history of the dance concert: how they grew from movers to dancers to choreographers and critics. "What are you learning from this experience?" prompts Ehrlich. "How might it shape your future work?"

Throughout this long process, Ehrlich's students have begun to understand what it is to think and work as choreographers. What this full-bodied experience has brought them is not a moment of insight into the world of dance, but the kind of mindfulness that emerges from nurturing and building complex understandings (Wolf and Pistone in press). These students are all developing the same understandings and habits of mind that sustain and enhance the work of professional choreographers. But they are also learning important lessons about taking responsibility for their work, about establishing a way of working and thinking and presenting their own ideas, about what it takes to pursue a project over time, and what it takes to get better.

There is nothing sacrosanct about an example drawn from dance. One can be a real-world apprentice in writing, or carry out experiments in chemistry, or do original-source research in history. What makes these kinds of experiences so powerful is that they remain central to the discipline and relevant beyond the school walls. These experiences do not test students for what they know; they test students for what they understand. In that way, assessment stands not separate from, but in combination with, instruction and learning as part of an educational process that reaches far beyond the doorstep of the classroom.

Developing Reflection as a Habit of Mind

Though the goal of general education may not be to churn out professional choreographers, playwrights, scientists, or mathematicians, we hope that students will come to see themselves as active, thoughtful, independent learners. Yet, standardized tests displace students from the process and responsibility of assessment. Instead, these tests subject students to evaluative measures whose norm-referenced, numerical scores cannot capture the kinds of reflective processes students engage as active learners generating work, tending ideas, and developing a way of thinking in a given domain. If authentic assessment is intended, as we think it should be, to reveal students' understandings, then we must find measures that capture the hidden aspects and processes that lie in, around, under, and behind students' work.

As our dance example implied, students' accomplishments are as deeply rooted in the creation as in the completion of their work.

Students' abilities to confront these kinds of real-world challenges—to understand their work in relation to that of others, to build on their strengths, to see new possibilities and challenges in their work—all depend on their capacity to step back from their work and consider it carefully, drawing new insights and ideas about themselves as young learners. This kind of mindfulness grows out of the capacity to judge and refine one's work and efforts before, during, and after one has attempted to accomplish them: precisely the goal of reflection. Nonetheless, the practice of reflection is profoundly lacking in most school settings—and in virtually all forms of traditional testing measures. In how many classrooms are students asked to engage in forms of self-assessment that help them examine the many steps, choices, and decisions that guided them in the development of their work? It is even harder to find classrooms where students are asked to take responsibility for carefully judging their own growth and development.

Here is an example of a classroom in which students are indeed asked to take on the practice and responsibility of assessing their own work. Jerry Halpern teaches 9th grade English at Langley High School in Pittsburgh. Halpern states:

> I want my classroom to be student centered. Well, what does that mean? It means that the major focus must be on reflection. If students are to be more self-directed, then they have to be able to judge and look at their own work. Reflection is the essential activity that brings about those skills (J. Halpern, personal communication, June 1990).

As Halpern implies in his comments, although reflection encourages (and provides concrete evidence of) students' development as active learners, it is a demanding practice. First, it demands from teachers and students a commitment to the habit and practice of looking back in order to forge ahead. In Halpern's class, reflection is granted a status beyond that of a classroom activity to a habit of mind, a basic skill for working and thinking as a writer. In this classroom, reflection is a regular and frequent practice that takes many forms:

• Students keep logs, in which they track their daily progress, reporting and describing what they did, as well as noting comments and thoughts about the various decisions and choices they made as writers.

• Students engage in lively classroom discussions, in which they share their work, ponder possible strategies for improving it, make judgments and distinctions about what they like and dislike, and determine what makes one piece powerful and riveting and another dull and uninteresting.

• Students participate in lengthy peer response sessions and interviews. Here they hone their skills for making thoughtful judgments and posing challenging questions about the work and process of writing.

• Students are given opportunities to write formal reflections, in which they review their past work and begin to develop a sense of their growth and learning over time.

As evidence of what can be learned from incorporating students' reflections, we share one example of reflection in action. (For further reference, see Seidel and Zessoules 1990.) Scott is a student in Halpern's classroom. As part of his work on a play-writing project, Scott is being challenged to carefully consider his work and make sense of his endeavors as a new playwright. Scott's full-bodied experience with writing plays is immediately apparent when one reads his reflections in conjunction with his scenes and dialogues. Taken together, these pieces create a vivid picture of Scott as a young playwright. In one of his early reflections, Scott talks candidly about his role and responsibility as a playwright and the importance of having a real audience:

> It made me happy that the class enjoyed my scene. After all, isn't that what it's all about? Pleasing the audience. I'd rather write something that makes the people watching it happy than write something technically good that the class doesn't really get into (Alpert 1990).

Absorbed in his role as a new playwright, and mindful of the many possibilities in writing plays, Scott points directly to his chosen challenge: to write comic theater. Given this perspective, Scott demands a new and different kind of attention to his work. In effect, he is telling us how to read his work: what to look for, what to pay attention to, and what to question in it. He is working to gain insight into what makes a scene funny, keeping in mind his chosen audience and anticipating the added dimensions and qualities of performance.

Scott works steadily on this challenge and fills his folder with comic sketches, scenes, and dialogues. At the end of the sequence, he looks back over his work to see how successfully he has achieved his goals:

> My approaches changed, but my style always stayed the same. I've tried to be humorous the whole sequence. In the beginning, I thought of the most ridiculous scenes. I tried anything to be funny and now that I look back on it, it was weak. . . . Now when I write scenes, I always try to do them real-life and be humorous at the same time. . . . A playwright has a tough job. It's not easy to come up with a good scene. . . . If I knew someone just starting to write plays, my advice would be: Write about real-life experiences. Have solid characters, don't make their

attitudes change line-by-line. Try to be funny. Have some conflict or tension. And, most important, . . . have fun. Just relax and have a lot of fun doing the scenes. Also keep the audience in mind. Write a scene to please yourself and also one that will please your audience (Alpert 1990).

Scott has come a long way in discerning exactly what makes a scene funny, by directly confronting the issues and problems central to his chosen challenge. Through experimenting with different approaches to humor, he has come to better understand the particular qualities and characteristics of comedy.

Scott's ability to thoughtfully tackle the complex craft of writing plays grows out of his capacity to judge and refine his work and efforts over time. Yet, all of these understandings risk remaining hidden without the added dimensions captured by his reflections and self-assessments. And that is where Halpern steps back into the picture. While his students' reflections and self-assessments create one piece of the assessment puzzle, Halpern's perceptions of his students' efforts are required to complete the picture. Halpern's commitment to the practice of reflection and self-assessment means that there will be no quiz or final exam to test his students' achievement or their burgeoning understandings resulting from their work as young playwrights. Instead, his student's work itself will be the basis for assessment, and Halpern must find a way into that work to observe, document, and assess the multiple, often invisible, dimensions of his students' understandings. To do this, Halpern turns to students' reflections:

I really believe that reflection is the key that allows the teacher to unlock the picture of students' growth. You can see some change in their writing, but to get the total picture, you must have their reflections. And this is what really opens up the dimensions for assessment to a much broader range of skills that may not have been in your lesson plans. It's more complicated than grading. You see, in grading we often tend to think in terms of "the facts": Did they do the assignment? Do they have the proper heading? Is it neat? Those are the facts; and we assign A, B, C, or D. But the way we've been talking about assessment, it's not about the facts; it's about learning skills. In the drama project, we are assessing student's understanding of a particular art form. You have to accept whatever lesson comes out for the student, and this lesson may not be in your handbook. Be ready for surprises. When students are doing all this writing, and they have all of these reflections, they have created a body of work that they can identify with. There's no predicting where these new understandings may take them or you (J. Halpern, personal communication, June 1990).

Halpern's classroom is only one example of how reflection plays a critical part in revealing the multiple layers of students' understanding. When students and teachers make use of reflection as a tool for learning and assessment, they are creating an opening that allows them to enter into students' work, making sense of their endeavors and accomplishments, and learning how they judge their success. As Halpern said, there is no predicting just how far these new understandings may take you. It is precisely this revelation of new understandings, this habit of reflection, that has the power to boost the silent and mechanistic approach to assessment into an active, vivid discourse between teachers and students. It is this habit of mind that marks one of the most vivid distinctions between a testing culture and an assessment culture in the classroom.

Documenting Students' Evolving Understandings

Powerful assessment measures should reveal more than what students know and understand. Powerful assessment must also capture how those new understandings metamorphose. In this way, assessment serves as evidence of students' evolving strengths and weaknesses. Assessment reveals how students' capacities to solve sophisticated problems, make sensitive judgments, and complete complex projects broaden and deepen over time. Yet, at this point in most school settings, little has been done to carefully document the subtle nuances of students' development. The dominance of standardized testing has rendered schools ill equipped to focus on transformations in students' development. Norm-referenced, numerical scores do not yield detailed information about how a student has changed relative to her younger self. Isolated test scores tell us little or nothing about the ripening of processes and understandings students engage in.

We examine one example of how authentic assessment, in the form of student "process-folios," or selected works showing the development of students' learning over time, can be used to powerfully enrich the portrait of students' changing abilities and the picture of daily teaching practices. Norman Brown teaches visual arts at Schenley High School in Pittsburgh. For the past four years, Brown has been experimenting with Arts Propel process-folios in his art classes. The visual arts has a long and rich tradition associated with student portfolios, Propel process-folios differ from the traditional conception. First, unlike a traditional portfolio, which houses a select sample of highly polished works, process-folios contain a range in variety and quality of works chosen to show the depth, breadth, and growth of student's thinking. Beyond introducing readers to the new understandings and practices embedded in students' project work, process-folios provide an even richer opportunity for learning and assessment in that they are intended to document the evolution of new understandings over time and across many projects—those that were satisfying and those that were not.

A sample process-folio from one student includes the various notes, thumbnail sketches, detailed studies, and journal excerpts that tell the story of the development of his cubist piece on African masks. He also includes a color study, several cartoons, a sculpture, and a series of works investigating issues of composition, texture, and perspective. Taken together, these pieces sample the terrain he has covered in his studies. In addition, this particular student has chosen several early works and reflections, as well as excerpts from a portfolio interview, to illustrate the emergence of his style by comparing the stages of his development over time.

Process-folios like this one reveal the multiple dimensions of learning that Brown wishes to capture. These dimensions include the development of his students' expertise and the evolution of generative shifts in his students' understandings in comparison to their younger selves. But Brown is adamant in stating that these patterns of growth and change are complex and do not always follow a linear or monotonic progression. Therefore, the creation of process-folios in the classroom requires constant monitoring, not only to document but to reflect on new insights, directions, and possibilities in student work. This work takes time because the growth Brown wants to see goes further than the mastery of technique and media; he wants to delve into students' capacities to find new ways of expressing themselves, showing that they know how to think as visual artists. The key, according to Brown (1989), is committing to the long-term practice of building student process-folios:

> The single most important constant in my classroom is the portfolio review. While this may originally have occurred once or twice throughout a semester, it now occurs on a continual, on-going basis. It has become very much a part of every student evaluation, as well as something students are taught to do for themselves. Portfolio review may begin with a student laying out every piece of work done over a week, a month, or a semester. We may do this as a class, using a critique format, or individually, face-to-face, teacher and student (p. 8).

What emerges from these kinds of classroom conversations is a common language, allowing Brown and his students to share a compelling vision of assessment and learning—one that respects the full range of his students' skills and understandings. Consequently, the act of reviewing a student's process-folio becomes an articulation of a student's growth and learning: a unique blend of instruction, learning, and assessment. In this light, the shared insights and understandings that emerge from the examination of student process-folios become a critical component of the classroom culture.

To keep track of students' explorations and discoveries, Brown's students are required to record notes in journals or on papers attached to the back of their works. He asks them to jot down what they like and don't like; what changes they might make in the piece; how they judge that work; what they think they learned from it. The students take this work seriously: when they review in a process-folio, each piece of work can be subject to scrutiny. In a process-folio, each piece of work, no matter how trivial, messy, or incomplete, may be full of clues to the student's development as a young artist and an active learner (Brown 1989).

Brown's testimony is thought provoking:

> Revisiting and reworking "old ideas" often produces brilliant leaps of insight in the minds of young art students. Through the close examination of portfolios, students begin to trace their convoluted journey, noting where ideas, experiments and works seem to zigzag, watching themes develop and solidify. The "footprints" of the journey begin to make sense. . . . Where does this lead us? I see what used to be a 45 minute traditional art class becoming an enthusiastic studio environment, where the students and teacher create living portfolios. A studio classroom can be rich with perception and the sharing of ideas through reflection, ultimately leading students to the personal rethinking of their own final products. In this environment students may create "footprints" that are not washed away in some quick wave, but rather provide a map of their own "waves of thinking," for their minds, hand and eyes to follow (Brown 1989, p. 11).

As Brown's comments suggest, capturing students' evolving understandings is central to the development of active learners. This kind of "living" documentation is also a vital consideration for any model of authentic assessment.

Assessment as a Moment of Learning

The notion that assessment can—and should—be used to provoke further learning (or to inform instruction), stands far beyond the usefulness of standard assessment practices. Too often, assessment is treated as separate and distinct from learning and instruction. Instead, assessment is an activity designated typically for either end of the learning process: done before students start learning, to determine what they don't know, or after they have finished learning, to determine what (or how much) they have learned. As we have already observed, authentic assessment has the potential to accommodate fuller, more dynamic evaluations of student understanding, because it has the power to integrate assessment with learning and instruction. But these processes will continue to function purely as evaluative vehicles if they are simply tucked in at the ends of semesters as placement for final exams. Assessment, no matter how authentic its measures might be, cannot simply be inserted into the classroom.

The priorities in an authentic assessment environment highlight the importance of complex processes and understandings, rather than multiple products and basic knowledge. Consider the goals in the classrooms of Ehrlich, Halpern, and Brown. As their students work to choreograph original dances, discover the art of writing plays, or create rich portfolios documenting their growth as a visual artist, they are being challenged to continually make use of these experiences as powerful instances of learning. These students are challenged to do the following:

1. Tackle project work regularly and frequently. These students don't create one dance phrase, write one dramatic scene, or paint one family portrait and then move on to the next unit. They produce many works, exploring many aspects of the given discipline.

2. Judge their own work—not once or twice, but again and again, as it is in progress, finally completed, or in relation to earlier and later works.

3. Collaborate and converse with others, not as simply an interesting switch of pace, but as a critical element of working and thinking as active learners discussing, sharing, and learning from others' perceptions.

4. Distinguish a real audience for their work beyond the classroom teacher—challenging them to reflect on the intent and purpose of their work.

5. Picture their learning and development over time again, not only at the end of the year, but also across the weeks, months, and even years of their academic careers.

6. Understand what it means to get better—helping them to develop and strive for standards of excellence and performance.

In this setting, students are continually engaged in explorations of ways of knowing that are self-initiated and self-sustained. Classrooms become, as Brown (1989) has suggested, studios, labs, or workshops for immersing oneself in genuine work, thus setting the stage for authentic assessment as part of an ongoing, educational process.

Like the particular qualities associated with a testing culture, authentic assessment doesn't automatically happen in the classroom. As Ehrlich, Halpern, and Brown will testify, it is not enough to have compelling projects, reflective activities, and fat portfolios in the classroom. Teachers must commit not only to the variety of activities and opportunities associated with authentic assessment, but to making use of these activities and to being affected by them and by the understandings and insights they yield. These practices must be seen as potentially fertile resources that are intended to be shared, extended, returned to, and built on to provoke further learning. Otherwise, students' experiences with them risk becoming dry, hollow, and mechanistic. In effect, the work of authentic assessment must itself be learned. An assessment culture means that teachers and students are continually asking themselves, "How can I make use of this knowledge and feedback?" To that end, the complex practices and processes involved in authentic assessment require a great deal of time and effort both within the classroom walls and beyond. Teachers must ask themselves: "How long does it take to nurture students' habits of mind? When is it appropriate to assess students' work? What kinds of qualities should I look for initially? How might those dimensions change over time? How do I document the broadening of these skills and abilities?"

The answers to these questions do not come easily. On a practical level, things happen slowly in an assessment culture. Students cannot be marched quickly through the curriculum, because it is not composed of a series of activities that yield discrete products, but rather a set of opportunities that encourage complex habits of mind, ways of working, and processes of learning. These processes mature and develop in an ongoing, if bumpy, way. The key is to commit to the ongoing process as an essential tool in students' development. The nurturing relationship between the teacher as master and student as apprentice does not come as a result of one two-week classroom project. Instead, it is made up of small successes rather than major breakthroughs, and it must be nurtured and allowed to unfold over time (Howard 1990).

* * *

In summary, authentic assessment involves a complicated reevaluation of classroom activities and responsibilities, transforming the classroom along many dimensions: changing the kinds of activities students engage in on a daily basis; altering the responsibilities of students and teachers in increasingly sophisticated ways; and transforming the static, mechanical, and disengaging moments when learning stops and testing begins into a continuum of moments that combine assessment, instruction, and learning. By integrating assessment into the day-to-day classroom experience, one changes its role dynamically. No longer a weapon for rooting out and combatting students' weaknesses, assessment becomes an additional occasion for learning—a tool for students, as much as for teachers, parents, and administrators to discover strengths, possibilities, and future directions in students' work. In this way, students are actively involved in an ongoing, educational process, capitalizing on the processes of authentic assessment to move forward in their work as active learners.

Now that we have laid the foundation for these practices, we will consider what it takes to implement them in the classroom.

Authentic Assessment in Action

Putting authentic assessment practices into action requires a profound shift of the responsibilities and roles for students, teachers, and administrators. The remainder of this chapter explores the scope and impact of the key practices on the following audiences:

1. *Students as active participants in the process of assessment.* As students take on increased responsibility for their own learning and assessment, their growing awareness and ownership of their development enables them to make use of the process of assessment as a tool for learning.

2. *Teachers as reflective practitioners.* Teachers, who traditionally judge students' work against their own or other mandated standards, are now encouraged to become accomplished coaches in the process of self-assessment. To do so, teachers, like students, must immerse themselves in the practice of reflection.

3. *School administrators as key advocates for authentic assessment.* Very few, if any, of these changes will occur without the commitment and dedication of school administrators. Institutional support is fundamental to the process of assessment. Educators cannot expect to benefit from the rich

knowledge generated by authentic assessment if they do not sustain the practices that make it a reality.

Students as Active Participants in Assessment

Perhaps the most dramatic shift is that of the roles and responsibilities of students themselves. The work at the heart of an assessment culture requires students to alter their perceptions of themselves as active learners. Authentic assessment challenges students to become thoughtful judges of their own work. Theirs is the work of posing questions, making judgments, integrating criticisms, reconsidering problems, and investigating new possibilities. With this work comes the responsibility of assessment. Students must educate themselves to become accurate evaluators of their own efforts. They must come to recognize and build on the strengths in their work and to diagnose and treat their weaknesses. No longer the passive subjects of testing and evaluation, students are key players in the process of assessment.

As an example of emerging reflectiveness on a student's own work, consider Tony, a 9th grader immersed in the middle of a play-writing project in an English class at Langley High School in Pittsburgh. Tony has written five dialogues so far, his first since 6th grade, when he wrote dialogues to practice quotation marks. When asked, at this midpoint in his project, to review his writing, Tony had this to say:

> I feel like my writing has formed 2 hills, like this.

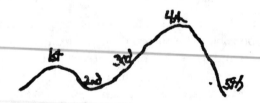

> I was writing good, to my standards, then it started lacking what I thought made it good. Then I started climbing again, this time greater than my first one. Finally, my last dialogue was terrible (Seidel 1989, p. 6).

Tony's reflection provides a powerful portrait depicting the hills and valleys of his development as a young writer. As he wends his way from novice to journeyman to student expert, Tony takes on the responsibility of following and defining the confusing ups and downs of his work. With time and practice, Tony will be able to articulate more about his successes and failures and his evolving sense of goals and standards; he will tell us what delights him, what compels him, what falls short of his expectations, and what rings true in his work.

Tony's ability to picture his own growth and learning over time is a vital component of authentic assessment. His growing awareness and ownership of his development are a first step in enabling him to make use of assessment as a moment of learning—helping him to define excellence and competence, strengths and weaknesses, and challenges and goals in the work of writing plays. Tony is developing the same habits of mind that sustain and enhance the work of professional playwrights (Seidel 1989). As he continues to write dialogues and scenes, Tony will also be developing his ability to act as his own judge in order to construct and convey his understanding of writing plays. This is the work of authentic assessment. In a very real sense, Tony is an apprentice learning to nurture complex understandings; to confront and embrace the ongoing processes of assessment; to be mindful of his own development; and, perhaps most important, to develop the habit of reflection.

Teachers as Reflective Practitioners

The shift in students' responsibilities may be a dramatic one, but it is not a magical transformation. The changes in students' roles and responsibilities require a parallel shift in teachers' own roles and responsibilities. Whereas a testing culture promotes the notion of a teacher-centered classroom, an assessment culture requires a student-centered classroom. In effect, authentic assessment requires teachers to step back from their traditional roles at the head of the classroom, allowing students to take center stage and teachers to become accomplished guides in the process of self-assessment. It is this act of stepping back that enables teachers to practice and infuse the habit of reflection into their own pedagogical approach. In this light, teachers become researchers in the classroom, posing central questions to better inform their sense of students' learning, their approach to teaching strategies, and the development of their own reflective habits. Just as authentic assessment asks students to develop the habit of pausing to

reflect in order to move forward, so, too, must teachers adopt the
practice of taking time to stop and think, to observe and make sense of
the activities and progress of their students.

Carolyn Olasewere, a 10th grade English teacher at Westinghouse
High School in Pittsburgh, piloted the Propel play-writing project. She
talks here about her transformation as she practices the fine art of
stepping back from the front of the classroom. Her comments are titled
"The Metamorphosis of O" (O being the initial of her last name):

> I hate to think of myself as a big bug! I run what you could call a very
> teacher-centered classroom. I'm on stage. But doing this project
> changed my perception of everything! I actually turned my classroom
> over to my students. They were in charge. I was more of a facilitator.
> But that didn't mean I wasn't actively involved. I was extremely busy,
> being more flexible but more organized—keeping my finger on the
> pulse of all of this activity. Surprisingly I found they could handle it.
> Even more, I found I could handle it. Plus, I discovered I had a much
> better idea of them and the processes they were going through. I felt
> a special relationship was developing. Students found me more
> approachable and they became much more willing to voice questions,
> ideas, frustrations, and doubts. The change in me was really affective,
> feeling and finding the growing relationship and coming to better
> understand students' learning as a result (Olasewere 1989).

As Olasewere's role changes, her responsibilities also evolve. As her
students take on the work of learning and assessment, her work becomes
that of keen observer, coach, and expert in the workshop. Olasewere
has come to view her students as young writers, growing, advancing,
and maturing in their craft—rather than as students "doing a unit."
Repositioning herself so that she can observe, coach, and note
developments in student work becomes essential to Olasewere's new role
as facilitator. Part of what makes Olasewere such an expert coach is her
refined sense of how to respond to students' efforts, knowing when to
step in to activate a perplexed or wayward student and when to step back
to allow for the process of discovery. Teachers like Olasewere, who are
committed to the process of authentic assessment, develop the fine art of
stepping back to work side by side with students. In this way, teachers
send an important message that they not only can inform and instruct,
but also can respect and admire students' capabilities.

This clinical form of assessment involves continuous monitoring
and diagnosing of students' work and learning. It requires teachers to
carefully consider the broad scope of activities, knowledge, and
understanding that is being constructed in their classrooms. What should

they look for? When do they look? And how precisely can they name what they see students are learning? The act of questioning to inform teaching practice is central for teachers committed to an assessment culture in their classroom.

Another teacher, Jerry Halpern (introduced in a previous section), kept a running log of his thoughts, perceptions, and observations, in an attempt to capture his own reflective process during the play-writing project. Dubbed "The Captain's Log," these notes recorded Halpern's reflections on several aspects of classroom activities, including students' writing, students' written reflections, and the dynamics of classroom activities. Halfway through the project, Halpern shares his confusion:

> There is so much going on here that I feel a little out of control. Am I focusing enough on specific skills? Am I giving enough positive reinforcement? They seem to be making changes in dialogues and scenes as a result of rehearsal—but I don't have a handle on the type and significance of the changes—why are they making them? Are they improvements? They do seem to be having fun (J. Halpern, quoted by Seidel 1989, p. 9).

Through his questions, Halpern creates a vivid picture of his class of young writers. At the same time, he acknowledges his difficulty in discerning exactly what his students are learning. Just as Halpern is asking his students to confront the issues and problems central to the craft, he too must come to understand the particular qualities and characteristics of writing plays. Halpern must do this to better observe and evaluate what, indeed, his students are learning. Implicit in this belief is the need for teachers like Halpern and Olasewere to educate and question themselves and be open to new possibilities and understandings of the criteria for assessing the development of student work in a particular discipline.

Toward the end of the drama project, Halpern records these thoughts:

> As for the project, I'm not sure about the degree of success but I do know students worked consciously, diligently, and willingly at the activities: they wrote scenes and dialogues. They revised based on their rehearsals. They worked collaboratively to put the scenes together. They assumed the roles of playwright, actor, and director. They criticized and accepted criticism. They adapted to each other's idiosyncrasies. They shared their thoughts and work. They thought and wrote about what they were doing. They helped one another. They recognized strengths and weaknesses in themselves and others and

modified their actions to deal with them. They sacrificed their egos and performed (Seidel 1989, p. 9).

Halpern has come a long way in defining what his students are learning. Though he still may not have definite answers, Halpern has been able to unlock assessment in such a way that he can seriously consider the real work of students' endeavors as young playwrights. He has done this by taking on the role of keen observer and coach and by educating himself about what it means to be an expert. In so doing, Halpern has taken important steps in terms of his own growth and professional development.

In an assessment culture, teachers must immerse themselves in reflective assessment practices, both as experts in the classroom and as professionals in the field. Teachers cannot coach authentic assessment unless they themselves engage and value it in their own profession, and unless they themselves have some sense of how to convey that understanding to others. Thus, this process, like any other effective teaching, involves both the practice of reflection itself and the knowledge of how to engender that mindfulness in others.

Administrators as Key Advocates for Authentic Assessment Practices

There is ultimately a need to validate authentic assessment in the classroom by bridging it to systemwide (or even nationwide) accountability. The institutionalization of authentic assessment ensures that this work in the classroom will not erode away. In the same way that the implementation of authentic assessment inherently transforms the climate and practices of the classroom, institutionalizing authentic assessment must inevitably change the habits, structure, and policies of schools themselves. To bring about such change, educators must be prepared to confront many challenges:

1. *Teachers must be allowed to incorporate the practices of authentic assessment in their classrooms.* Teachers and administrators must find ways to work creatively with established policies and standard operating procedures to support and encourage changes in the art, practice, and profession of teaching and assessing students. The implementation of authentic assessment practices involves compromise. On a practical level, many teachers find themselves caught between the requirements of the mandated curriculum on the one side and the requirements of authentic assessment practices on the other. Teachers committed to the process of

authentic assessment may find themselves in direct opposition to dictates of the school principal, departmental supervisors, the school board, or other district administrators. Yet, unless teachers are given opportunity and encouragement to engage in and experiment with authentic assessment practices in their classrooms, it will be virtually impossible to change our vision of assessment and learning.

2. *School administrators must find ways to support teachers as reflective professionals working together to confront the issues at the heart of authentic assessment.* The education of teachers' own sensitivities and sensibilities around the issues of authentic assessment cannot be done in isolation. Authentic assessment sets a context for evaluating students as active learners; at the same time, authentic assessment demands that teachers be viewed as professionals in the work of teaching and assessing. This work requires critical opportunities for teachers to work and reflect collaboratively with fellow colleagues to better understand and appreciate their own efforts and endeavors. This work is complex, and it involves developing a common language for discussing learning and assessment so that teachers can make connections, share experiences, and use their expertise, not only from project to project, but from class to class, teacher to teacher, and year to year. The work of authentic assessment must acknowledge, educate, and enhance teachers' expertise and professional development as much as it does the work of students. The Arts Propel project has created several models for teachers and administrators to serve in assessment groups supporting one another over several years. Other long-running projects, like the Lincoln Center Institute, have also evolved methods for teachers, professional artists, and administrators to work together over significant periods of time.

3. *Educators must elicit support from the widest possible audience for assessment.* Another crucial component in this equation is the link to parents and the surrounding community. Educators concerned with school reform must find ways of informing and incorporating the concerns and enthusiasm of the community to enlist support and propagate acceptance of new forms of assessment.

4. *Educators must confront pressures for accountability.* Institutionalization inevitably raises the issues and problems of accountability. The impact of authentic assessment in the classroom is far reaching. Yet, the notion that authentic assessment can occur solely within the confines of the classroom is severely limiting. At its very best, the practice of authentic assessment will cause radical reforms in our conception of learning and evaluation. But, in all the excitement and possibilities generated by

authentic assessment, we cannot afford to romanticize its impact. Authentic assessment does not eradicate, but in fact inherits, many of the problems of standardized testing. Educators still need to confront issues of cultural bias, teacher fairness, validity, and reliability. To protect the integrity of authentic assessment, we need to engage in thoughtful, ongoing conversations to determine what we gain and lose by making authentic assessment part of rigorous, high-stakes accountability.

Although these are all genuine obstacles in the work of authentic assessment, the work of thoughtful educators is to prevent these difficulties from obscuring the strengths of this approach.

Conclusion

We have sought to describe some of the limits of the testing culture that is endemic in the United States and to outline an alternative assessment culture that could be adopted in the future. It is our view that the process of assessment is vastly more complex than the singular act of testing. Assessment is more than the development of better tests; it is in fact dependent on a whole network of classroom practices. These practices can be derived from investigating questions like "What are we looking for when we assess students' learning? What do we want students to know and understand? What kind of classroom culture nurtures the development of these understandings? And how can these practices be used to inform teaching and assessment?" In this way, daily classroom practice does indeed drive instruction and learning.

On careful examination, the culture behind authentic assessment is very sensitive; therein lies its power and its vulnerability. If we, as thoughtful educators, want to be rigorous about reform, then we cannot depend on the ripple effects caused by merely changing the kinds and qualities of testing in our schools. Instead, we must be committed to building a foundation to support and sustain the practice of more authentic forms of assessment. The adoption of authentic assessment in American schools may not be easy and is unlikely to happen unless, as Wiggins (1989) suggests, such instruments are seen as essential alternations of current nonadaptive procedures. Authentic assessment must come to be seen as so essential that it "justifies disrupting the habits and spending practices of conventional school keeping" (p. 712).

In our view, the adoption of an assessment culture depends first on the active involvement of students and teachers. Further, unless teachers genuinely believe that these instruments are useful and that they can help them achieve their own pedagogical goals, authentic assessment instruments will never find their way off the closet shelves. Yet, even full-scale teacher support will not suffice. Equally important is the endorsement of school administrators and the belief and trust of parents and the wider community. The best hope for achieving such endorsement lies in setting up examples of authentic assessment; asking for support—on all levels—to sustain them; and then subjecting these models to discussion and scrutiny.

References

Alpert, S. (1990). [Unpublished journal entries].

Brown, N. (February 1989). "Portfolio Reviews: Pivots, Companions and Footprints." *Portfolio, The Newsletter for Arts Propel* 4: 8–11.

Gifford, B. (1990). *From Gatekeeper to Gateway*. Report on the National Commission on Testing and Public Policy. Chestnut Hill, Mass.: Boston College Press.

Howard, K. (Spring 1990). "Making the Writing Portfolio Real." *The Quarterly of the National Writing Project and The Center for the Study of Writing* 12, 2: 4–7, 27.

Mitchell, R. (October 1989). "A Sampler of Authentic Assessment: What It Is and What It Looks Like." Materials prepared for the 1989 Curriculum/Assessment Alignment Conferences, co-sponsored by the County State Steering Committee of the California Association of County Superintendents and the State Department of Education, Sacramento and Long Beach.

Neill, M., and N. Medina. (May 1989). "Standardized Testing: Harmful to Educational Health." *Phi Delta Kappan* 70, 9: 688–697.

Olasewere. C. (January 20, 1989). "The Metamorphosis of O." Discussion conducted at the meeting of the Arts Propel Drama Team, Pittsburgh.

Seidel, S. (December 1989). "Even Before Portfolios." *Portfolio, The Newsletter for Arts Propel* 4: 6–9.

Seidel, S., and R. Zessoules. (July 1990,). "Through the Looking Glass: The Practices of Reflection and Self-Assessment in a Language Arts Classroom." Paper presented at the Arts Propel Institute on New Modes of Assessment, Cambridge, Mass.

Wiggins, G. (May 1989). "A True Test: Toward More Authentic and Equitable Assessment." *Phi Delta Kappan* 70, 9: 703–713.

Wolf, D. (1989). "Artistic Learning as Conversation." In *Children and the Arts*, edited by D. Hargreaves, pp. 22–39. Philadelphia: Open University Press.

Wolf, D., and N. Pistone. (In press). "Taking Full Measure: Rethinking Assessment in the Arts." In *College Entrance Examination Board Monograph*. New York: College Entrance Examination Board.

Zessoules, R. (December 1989). "The Dance Marathon." *Portfolio, The Newsletter for Arts Propel* 4: 11, 14–19.

Zessoules, R., D. Wolf, and H. Gardner. (1988). "A Better Balance: Arts Propel as an Alternative to Discipline Based Art Education." In *Beyond DBAE: The Case for Multiple Visions of Art Education*, edited by J. Burton, A. Lederman, and P. London, pp. 117–130. North Dartmouth: Southeastern Massachusetts University Press.

6

The Rhetoric of Writing Assessment

Patricia Lambert Stock

During the 1987–88 academic year, four educators joined together to develop and teach an experimental 12th grade English course for students who were at risk of not graduating.[1] As teacher-researchers, our goal was to help students become more effective readers and writers and to plan, conduct, and report on an experimental process for evaluating students' reading and writing competency.

We designed the course, called *Inquiry and Expression*,[2] as an intensive reading and writing workshop built on a set of related questions that we hoped students would make their own:

- What has been the nature of your growing-up experiences?
- What are the stories you tell about them?
- What has been the nature of other individuals' growing-up experiences?
- What stories do they tell about their experiences?
- Are there common themes that characterize individuals' growing-up experiences or their growing-up stories?

Because we believe that individuals learn to read and write most effectively when they do so to learn about subjects and issues that interest them for purposes that are compelling to them, we encouraged each student to identify and investigate specific questions of interest to her, questions embedded or implied in the more general ones we had posed.

We planned three different but interrelated writing assessments that would provide meaningful information about the quality of students' learning to the three audiences to whom teachers and students are appropriately accountable: students, teachers and other professional

72

educators; and students' parents and other members of the local, state, and national communities who have vested interests in students' learning. Of course, the needs and interests of these groups differ. For our students' benefit, we planned for them to collect all their course writings in a portfolio that would serve as the basis for student-teacher conferences about their developing literacy; for our benefit and for the benefit of our professional colleagues, we developed interpretative case studies of our students' learning from the writings in their portfolios[3]; and for the benefit of people outside the schools, we arranged for our students to publish and distribute an anthology of their writing.

Building a Reading and Writing Course to Support Developing Literacy

At the heart of the *Inquiry and Expression* course were several planned occasions for improving reading and writing. In September and October, we provided students with a core of literary selections that we read aloud together and discussed in our classrooms. We introduced the growing-up theme by reading with students fiction, poetry, and essays composed by Asian Americans, African Americans, Hispanic Americans, and Native Americans. We did this to illustrate the variety of ways in which individuals can realize this theme in literary language and to dramatize the multicultural character and worldwide roots of the literature that Americans think of as their own. We also studied excerpts from Studs Terkel's *Hard Times* to show how one author inscribed stories that people tell about themselves and their lives. We listened to audiotapes of the interviews Terkel conducted and read both the monologues into which these interviews were transcribed by Terkel's secretary and the texts into which these transcriptions were inscribed by Terkel in his book.

After we began reading and discussing these selections together in class, we asked students to interview adults in their families, their neighborhoods, and the Saginaw community and record on audiotapes, in their own handwritten accounts, in letters written to them, and so on, the growing-up stories of the adults who have shaped their communities and their cultures. Using the stories they collected, we shaped lessons that asked students, for example, to transcribe talk, to inquire into the similarities and differences between spoken and written language, to speculate on the logic of the graphemic conventions of written texts, and to characterize the genres of speech and writing that they were rehearsing and composing.

From late October through January, we created a workshop setting in our classes. We asked students to work independently or in small groups to investigate themes or issues each had identified as particularly interesting during our first two months' work together.[4] Specifically, we asked students to read and write about three full-length works of literature dealing with the themes they were exploring and to draft and revise three growing-up stories in which they also explored those themes. In individual conferences and in small groups, as thesis advisors might, we discussed with students the books they were reading, the compositions they were writing, the issues and problems they were addressing.

In February, we asked students to read a second set of core readings, readings about the adolescent experience by two psychologists, a professional educator, and a sociologist. We did this to encourage them to explore other genres in which they might express the insights they were gaining into their various topics of inquiry, to provide an opportunity for them to read complex texts from their perspective as experts on the subject of growing-up experiences and the stories people tell about them, and to initiate discussions of the common themes to be found in their specific stories.

In March, we asked student to shift their attention from collecting and composing growing-up stories to critiquing and analyzing those stories in the light of their reading. And we joined our students as students of their literature. Following this close reading and analysis of the research they had produced, our students selected from their work the compositions they believed best represented their growing-up experiences; then, using desktop publishing equipment, they revised and published those compositions in *The Bridge*, an anthology they subsequently distributed and sold.[5]

Developing Interrelated Assessments for Different Audiences and Purposes

We believe that reading and writing are complex, situated activities. We also believe that a valid assessment of students' reading and writing competencies is one that enables assessors to recognize and account for the complex ways in which students use reading and writing to make complex meanings in particular situations. A meaningful evaluation of students' literacy learning must itself be a complex, situated description of that learning composed to meet the particular interests and needs of the individuals to whom it is addressed. These convictions led us to base our three interrelated assessments not in samples but in all the writing that each student composed to fulfill the self-defined intellectual project she developed in the course. These writings, collected in portfolios by students, became the subject matter of our course and the materials of our assessments.

The arguments for portfolio assessments are well known to educators. Portfolios allow assessors to examine a body, rather than a sample, of students' work in order to judge the quality of that work. More important, though, the concept of portfolio assessment allows assessors to decide how the portfolios they will examine will be constructed and what functions their evaluations of those portfolios will serve. For example, those who would use portfolios to examine the quality of students' writing need to ask themselves what the portfolios will be composed of: The writings that students believe are their best work? Several pieces of writing and all the notes and drafts that led to their composition? Examples of different modes or styles of writing?

Discussing what goes into a portfolio invites educators to identify the qualities implicit in both effective writing and effective writing instruction, and to determine how the two relate to one another. Discussing the uses to which portfolios and their evaluations can be put may be similarly revealing: Will portfolios be constructed by students? By teachers? Will portfolio readings and evaluations be undertaken by students so that they may assess their own work? Will they be undertaken by teachers to determine students' course grades? And if so, will they be read by classroom teachers? By outside evaluators? By a team of classroom teachers and outside evaluators? Will students carry their portfolios with them from class to class or grade to grade? Will students ultimately select from their working/traveling portfolios to assemble capstone portfolios that figure in one way or another as exit/entrance examinations for different levels of schooling?

The possible shapes of portfolios are as various as the needs of those who would use them. In our course, we planned for students to collect all their written work in their portfolios for four reasons, three of which were related to the assessments we planned:

1. *We expected to develop our lessons from our students' writing.* We encouraged students to translate our instructional plans into their own terms and their own intellectual projects so that we could teach responsively and tailor lessons to their needs.

2. *We wanted each student's writing to serve as the occasion for individual student-teacher conferences.* In these conferences, we discussed the student's developing literacy within his or her specific intellectual project and within the general course of study.

3. *We planned to study the work in the portfolios in order to develop interpretative case studies of students' learning.* From other work we had done in assessment (Stock and Robinson 1987, Stock 1990), we knew that the most valid picture of students' writing competency is found in what Stephen M. North describes as the "meaningful, communicative" discourse they compose; we wanted to develop studies of such discourse that would reveal as much to interested educators about the interpretative nature of the assessment process as it does about the quality of students' writing.

4. *We planned for students to select from among their portfolio writings those they wished to develop and publish.* Numerical indicators are usually inadequate descriptions of the quality of students' literacy, so we planned for our students to offer the community a collection of literature they composed—literature that we believed the community would not only recognize as evidence of students' literacy but would also enjoy reading.[6]

Integrating Teaching, Learning, and Assessment

We began our work by asking students to write and discuss several informal compositions about growing-up experiences. During the first weeks of the course, Wendy Gunlock moved from rehearsing one of her grandmother's growing-up stories:

W-1
[The Outhouse][7]

I remember, it was rainy real hard & I had to go to the bathroom and back in my days we had to use the outhouses. Anyway I went out to use the outhouse to go to the bathroom & I was really tired that day because we had nothing to do because it was rainy so hard so I ran out to the outhouse & while I was waiting to the bathroom dozed off for about a 1/2 hour so my father was just getting his shoes on & when I woke up I hurried up & went in the house & my father said to me where in the hek were you. I was just getting my shoes on to look for you. We were getting worried. So I had told him that I fell asleep in the outhouse & he just started to laugh. They never let me forgot what happen.

to recalling times when she fought and played with her brother:

W-2
[My brother and I]

I remember when I was growing up, me and my brother would always get into fights. I remember one night my brother's friends, Scott & Jim was spending the night they snuk into my room & they had taped a tape of scary noises & when I fell asleep they snuk under my bed & pushed play & all I could her alnight was scarey noises so finally I got so scared I ran downstairs & into my mom & dads room & fell asleep in their bed I also remember we were getting our house rebuild & I was upstairs in my brother's room & I was jumping on his bed & a nail was sticking out & when I was jumping and the nail got stuck into my head & I went to bed not knowing about it & when I got up the next morning to comb my hair, the comb could not go all the way through my hair I went downstairs to ask my mom what was in my hair & she hurried up & got my dad up & took me to the hospital & they took the nail out & I don't remember if it even hurt.

to reviewing the good times she had during family motortrips:

W-3
[Family Traveling]

I remember when I was growing up, we did a lot of traveling. We had a lot of friends out of state (still do) and we would go & visit when we had a chance. We were in almost every state except for by up in Maine (them parts). It was really beautiful. We would drive through all the states & see all the sights. I remember driving through Kentucky, & the road we was on was out in the country, so all you could see was fields & some old houses with barns and horses. After we would drive through & get to our friends house, we would get settled and then go out driving around in their state that they lived in. It was a blast. Especially in West Virginia because my parents friend lives on a big hill & it issteep to. Anyway heir house was really hilly. It was great. I also liked driving through Florida because their friends would drive us along the beaches so we could see the oceans & condomens.

I Think I like Florida the best because it is hot, beautiful, & a lot of beaches. I have been to Florida about 5 to 10 times. The last 2 times I went to visit my brother & his wife to be, and we would also visit my parents frend Chris & Jewel who live in Pensecola. But every time I went I had a great time. So the point is. Try to get to see as much as the U. S. as possible, because there is so much to see.

to reconstructing narrative descriptions of her relationship to her parents and peers:

W-4
[Unrest at Home]

I remember when I was growing up about 3 people moved into my house when I was about 9 or 10. . . . Whenever something was missing, they would always ask us if we knew where it was. Of course, I did not know nothing about it, but [my mother's friend's kids] did, so they would say they didn't know even when they did. My mom & [her friend] would always say nobody is leaving till we know who took whatever was missing. [My mother's friend's kid] would always take things all the time. But I would get really mad because I couldn't leave the table because [he] would take it & he would always so he knew nothing about it. My mom would believe me, but I guess it didn't matter to much because I got yelled at & grounded. I was reall ticked off. Another time was when me & [he] got into a fight. It started out with me and my friend was outside sitting on the picnic table & [he] came out & threw some food at her, so I threw food back at him because he had no right throwing anything at my friends. So after that we got into a big fight & my mom & [her friend] came home & broke it up. We had to go in the house & tell them what happen, so I told them & [he] told his side & [my mom's friend] believed him & my mom believed me so she started to yell and she called me a Bitch so I took off & went over to my Dads for a couple of days. then her & my mom got into a big fight too, so she left for a couple days & my mom was really upset, but I didn't understand why she blamed me for starting it when he started it, plus he is always getting into trouble. Everything blew away though, I came back & so did [my mom's friend] & she said if we got into another fight she would ship me off to my dad's & [him] to his dad's. I was hoping she would because I wanted to live at my dads anyway.

Although liberally seasoned with mechanical and usage errors and expressed in language more characteristic of her speech than of our expectations for her writing, these compositions serve the purpose and fulfill the task we had assigned: to record growing-up stories that could be shared in class discussions—discussions we conducted to help students identify events, issues, people, or themes that they wanted to make the topic(s) of their reading and writing. Although we think she composed these first four writings to satisfy our own early assignments, not to explore her own intellectual project, we found in Wendy's willingness to "play school" indications both of her existing and potential capacities and of her sense of how to undertake writing tasks. Our analyses of Wendy's first four compositions show how we were looking at her writing in September and October 1987—through lenses shaped by a local assessment of student writing that we had worked together to develop the year before, through lenses worn by teachers who did not yet know Wendy, who were meeting her through writing she composed to fulfill their assignments. As Wendy learned how to shape her intellectual project, we learned how to read her texts, and the analyses that follow demonstrate teachers "keeping school." I include them here for two reasons: first, because they represent one kind of early reading that teachers make of student compositions (and often the only kind of reading that evaluators make); and second, because they provide a contrast to the readings of Wendy's texts that shape the bulk of this chapter.

Although the signals of phatic communion, the umms and ahs of oral storytelling, are deleted from it, Wendy's first piece of writing (W-1), written in one six-sentence paragraph, reads like a transcription of a story her grandmother told her. Assuming her grandmother's persona, Wendy begins her narrative: "I remember, it was rainy real hard & I had to go to the bathroom and back in my days we had to use the outhouses." Then, as if to signal the beginning of the dramatic action of the story, she asks readers to attend carefully, "Anyway. . . ." In so doing, Wendy seems to know that storytellers customarily provide their listeners or readers a context for the incident(s) that will shape the body of their stories, but she does not seem to know that a prefiguring reference in her first sentence (e.g., I remember a rainy day when I was young, back in the days when we had to use outhouses) or a backward glance from her second sentence to the first (e.g., One day I went out to use the outhouse . . .) would effect a more "literary" transition between these two parts of her story. While the last sentence of her paragraph, her grandmother's closing comment that "they never let me forget what happen," together with the opening one of the piece suggests that Wendy knows the dramatic action of stories customarily unfolds between an introduction (in this case contextual material) and a conclusion (in this case commentary), her introduction and conclusion are, at best, underdeveloped.

Further evidence that Wendy conceived her first piece of writing as a transcription of spoken language is found in the body of the narrative. Wendy organizes the piece chronologically: "I went out . . ."; "While I was waiting . . ."; "when I woke up. . . ." She tells the story, step by step, as it happened. Between the sentence-long introduction and the sentence-long conclusion that frame her piece, she marks typographically only four other sentences. In one of these (a 90-word sentence), she writes more than half her composition, using seven

coordinating conjunctions (&, so, &, so, &, &, &) and four subordinating
adverbs (*because, because, while, when*) to order and sequence the events; and
in so doing, she captures the rhythms of informal, spoken language. Her
use of the ampersand (&) and the subordinating conjunction *so* suggests
an effort to keep up with the tempo of the story she was hearing. And,
finally, she fails to mark the direct speech she composes in her
conclusion: ". . . where in the hek were you. I was just getting my shoes
on to look for you. We were getting worried." We did not specifically
draw Wendy's attention to the "oral" quality of her writing, but we did
engage her in class discussions about the differences between spoken and
written texts in a way that we hoped would enable her to recognize that
her first text read like a transcription of talk.

   Although Wendy begins her second piece (W-2) like her first, as if
in response to a request to recall a growing-up incident ("I remember
when I was growing up, me and my brother would always get into
fights."), this time she is the person doing the recalling; she does not
inscribe someone else's speech, she composes her own. This piece is
written in two long typographical sentences (one is almost 400 words),
and Wendy continues to make extensive use of the ampersand to relate
events to one another. (Her use of the conjunction *so* is almost absent
here; the one time she does use it, she uses it as a subordinating, not a
coordinating, conjunction: they played the "scary noises" so she "got
scared" and "ran downstairs.") We noted that Wendy might easily have
translated the run-on constructions in this piece into a number of
conventional sentences were she to replace the ampersands with more
conventional punctuation. But at the time she composed W-2, we
questioned whether Wendy understood the conventions for punctuation,
usage, and the arrangement of written language that would allow her to
coordinate, subordinate, or superordinate units of thought to one
another; therefore, we planned to raise our question with her when her
compositions provided specific textual occasions for doing so.

   When we first talked with Wendy about this second piece, we drew
her attention to the effectiveness of her overuse of detail to create
apparent danger: "snuk in my room," "taped scary noises," "snuk under my
bed," "all I could her alnight was scarey noises so finally I go so scared I
ran downstairs & jumped into my mom and dads room . . ."; and her
underuse of detail to express real danger: ". . . I was jumping and the nail
got stuck into my head & I went to bed not knowing about it . . . & they
took the nail out & I don't remember if it even hurt." We also contrasted
her second piece of writing with her first, pointing out the more effective

way in which she related the body of the second piece to its introduction. We noted to ourselves that the body of W-2 did not fulfill Wendy's introductory promise for it: the piece was not about fights with her brother, but about two frightening experiences in which she and her brother were involved. Our notation led us to add another lesson to the instructional plan we were developing for Wendy: when occasions presented themselves in class discussions or in writing conferences with her, we planned to invite her to illustrate generalizations with examples and to compose generalizations about examples. It was in this fashion in September that we read students' writing, tailoring our instructional plans with specific students in mind.

By the time Wendy submitted her third piece of writing, she had not only heard many of her classmate's stories about growing up, but read photocopies of several handwritten versions of these stories distributed for discussion in small groups and with the entire class. She had also read and heard read aloud the growing-up stories of published authors. These spoken and written narratives perhaps influenced the account of her family's motor trips (W-3); certainly we hoped they would. Composed in two paragraphs and 18 sentences, this piece has three exemplified generalizations and a one-sentence introduction that prepares the reader for what follows it. Furthermore, Wendy marks a difference between the significance of her visits to Florida and those to Kentucky and West Virginia by discussing her visits to Florida in a separate paragraph. Although the second paragraph might start more appropriately with the last sentence of the first paragraph, we were pleased that Wendy recognized that a new paragraph would communicate her meaning more effectively. Wendy also used commas for the first time to signal relationships of word units to one another within sentences, twice appropriately and twice inappropriately.

We found the weakest part of W-3 to be its two-sentence conclusion; Wendy's use of "So the point is"—like her use of "Anyway" in W-1—provided more evidence for our hypothesis that she was not able to—or not working to—consistently and effectively relate chunks of thought to one another. Wendy's writing also led us to ask whether she conceived her writer's task as that of pleasing the teacher, of simply meeting her assignments. We wondered if her use of "So the point is" signaled nothing more meaningful than her uncertainty about whether her narrative fulfilled an assignment. Did she sense that something general, something factual, should be offered to do so? Was hers a growing-up story? Should it have been something else—a travel log? An essay on the benefits of travel? On the greatness of America? After composing her own narrative, did Wendy wonder what uses it might have, what meanings it might communicate, in the school-world she occupied?

When Wendy composed the fourth and last piece she submitted to us in September (W-4), we were concluding our inquiry into the similarities and differences between speech and writing, the genres that contrast these two forms of language use, and the values that attach themselves to such contrasts in literate societies. We encouraged students to write about topics of concern to them in their own lives. Wendy responded with W-4, a narrative of personal experience whose topics contrast sharply with those in W-1, W-2, and W-3, a narrative that seems located not in a fixed past but a changing present. We had something new to which to respond, a new world to interpret.

Wendy's new text, our new text, had some old things in it: It is composed in one paragraph, and although its sentences are more consistently marked as such, its units of meaning cry out for shaped elaboration. It is characterized by inconsistent punctuation and usage—a persistent problem in Wendy's writing. Still, it has shape: an introduction, a body, a conclusion. Wendy offers a context for the incidents she narrates, though one that is underwritten if we are to judge the meaning of these incidents within it. She helps us understand their meaning by suggesting a mood that expresses her, not her teachers' presumed, reactions to the events she is telling: "I would get really mad"; "I guess it didn't matter to much"; "I was reall ticked off." And she provides a necessary resolution to her proffered dramatic incident, "Everything blew away though; I cam back and so did [my mom's friend].
. . ."

Most noteworthy perhaps is the conclusion. It is strikingly different from those in W-1 and W-3. W-1, for example, closes the narration in the past: "They never let me forgot what happen." W-3 closes even more surely with a piece of hortatory advice so general as to have no meaning in relation to personal experience: "So the point is. Try to get to see as much as the U.S. as possible, because there is so much to see." But in W-4, after giving post-closure to a narrated incident—"Everything blew away though; I came back and so did [my mom's friend]"— Wendy opens the discourse again using another of her characteristic ampersands:

> & she said if we got into another fight she would ship me off to my dad's & [him] to his dad's. I was hoping she would because I wanted to live at my dads anyway.

We had to read Wendy's next text to fully realize how open this ending was and is, and to gain a sense of what kind of opening it might prove to be. Textually, it does not work as well as some readers might want; intertextually, in our reading, it led us to speculate about Wendy's potential as a developing writer.

At this point in October, we had sense enough to read W-4, in spite of its problems, as Wendy's best writing, perhaps because in it she communicates something meaningful to us. Yet we did not ignore her problems because we knew that she had to grow to make texts that would be meaningful to others. In the conferences we had with Wendy about these first writings, pointing to specific passages in her texts, we discussed the reasons a writer might choose one word over another, one sentence design over another, one paragraph placement over another. We decided not to recommend particular choices to Wendy because we wanted her to develop the practice of thinking about language choices; we did not want her to form the habit of writing into her compositions every suggestion we made to her. Furthermore, we did not want to constrain Wendy's use of writing to shape an intellectual project of importance to her by narrowing her attention to focus on features of texts that she might more readily deal with later in the academic year.

Having introduced several themes in her writing during the first month of the course—her relationships to her parents, her relationships to her peers, and her family traveling experiences—Wendy used the next three months to explore these interrelated themes in her reading and in three essays, each of which she composed and revised over a month's time. For example, in W-5 Wendy accepted a curricular invitation of her own composing, the one in her opening closure of W-4: "I was hoping she would because I wanted to live at my dads anyway."

W-5
My Father

Me and my father were never really close or nor was he close to my brother, Steve. We would never really talk or do anything when he was sober, but when he was drunk, it seemed like we were the perfect family.

My father was an alcoholic, a bad one too. He would drink until he woke up untile he had to go to work. He woke up at around 11:00 am and he would leave for work at 2:00 pm. Then he would drink after he got out of work. He did this 6 days a week, and on Sunday we would just drink all day.

My father was an alcoholic for about three years, then he quit for about five years, until his dad died on my brother's birthday. Then he started drinking again. His drinking had been getting worse. Finally, one day I was outside with my cousin Kris playing ball. My parents were in the house talking. My mother called me in the house and told Kris to go home. When I came into the house I say my dad getting ready for work, when he left, he didn't give my mom a kiss good-bye like he use to.

My mom told me to sit down because she had to talked to me. When I sat down I asked her what was wrong. She said how would you feel about me and your father getting a divorce. I told her that I would be mad and I didn't want my dad to leave. I guess she never took in what I felt about them getting a divorce. While they were still separated, my moms friend moved in with her 2 kids. A boy and a girl.

While they were separated my dad had moved in with his mother. The divorce finally came through. They had been divorced for 7 or 8 years. When my dad moved out his drinking had been getting worse.

When my mom's friend moved in, me and my older brother never knew why until a couple of months later. They had been living with us for about 10 years. When I was older, because of the situation at my house I wanted to go and live with my father, but I wasn't sure if I wanted to live with an alcoholic. I never moved in with him, but I was scared to. So I never did.

When my brother was old enough to move out he signed up for the Navy. When I think about him joining the Navy, "I say to myself" He was the smart one.

I would always go over to see my dad on the weekends. I only say him once a week. I wanted to see more of him, but I couldn't because I got out of school at 3:00 pm and he would leave for work at 2:00 pm.

When I did visit him, all he did was drink. All day, beer after beer.

I remember one weekend I spent the night. Of course, he was drinking. It got to be so bad, that he opened a beer, drank half and he struggled to go to the refridgerator to get another. So he had 2 beers. I got up poured both cans down the drain. I was so upset I left his house around 1:00 am and went back home. After that incident I went back over there the day after. When I arrived he was still sleeping. When he woke up, he never knew that I had left.

His drinking became so bad, my mom and her friend took my dad into the hospital because of his drinking and he had a bad back. When we took him in the hospital he was drunk. Ever time I went to the Hospital, he would be asleep. When he was better, we took him out of St. Lukes and transfered him to community Hospital, hoping that if he was in a alcoholism center he would stop drinking. he was in community for a month. I would go and visit him every day. He would show me around & we would just talked. That was the first we evr had a conversation. When he got to leave the hospital, I finally got up the nerve to tell him how proud I was for him to stop drinking. When I told him, he said that drinking is very dangerous. It can kill you & it almost killed me.

Ever since he got out of the Hospital, he hasn't touched a drop of alcohol. It has been about a year since he drank. Now all he drinks is pop & coffee. I am so happy that he quit. Now his life is back together & even though he doesn't have my mom, but he does have a son and daughter who loves him very much.

This well-developed essay is the product of 8 to 12 hours of writing, discussion, and revision. It is an example of the quality of writing Wendy was composing by November. Its global organization is effective and serves Wendy's purpose: to describe her father from the perspective of her lived life as his daughter. In the first paragraph, she expresses straightforwardly, without self-pity, a sad reality: "Me and my father were never really close or nor was he close to my brother, Steve." In a second paragraph, she tells why she was unable to be close to her father: he "was an alcoholic, a bad one," and she elaborates on her definition of a bad alcoholic. In a third paragraph, continuing with the elaboration she has begun, she gives a history of her father's alcoholism. Beginning in the fourth paragraph, she dramatizes the effect of her father's alcoholism on the life of her family, indicating her reaction when her mother asks her how she would feel about her parents' separation and divorce: "I told her that I would be mad and I didn't want my dad to leave." With the understatement we have seen before in her writing (W-2), Wendy reflects: "I guess she never took in what I felt about them getting a divorce."

In three more paragraph-length units, Wendy describes the implications of the divorce for her father, her mother, her brother, and herself. In the 8th, 9th, and 10th paragraphs, she describes her weekend visits with her alcoholic father, and she dramatizes an especially painful one. In an 11th paragraph, she accounts for the crisis that leads to her father's hospitalization for alcoholism, her daily visits to see him, and the first real conversation they ever had. With poignant understatement, Wendy inscribes her effort to define her relationship with her father: "When he got to leave the hospital, I finally got up the nerve to tell him how proud I was for him to stop drinking." Similarly, she records her father's effort to build a relationship with her: "When I told him, he said that drinking is very dangerous. It can kill you & it almost killed me." As reflective readers, we heard a generalization like her previous 'Try to get to see as much as the U.S. as possible, because there is so much to see." Yet how differently grounded these new words are.

In a final paragraph, Wendy concludes her essay with a summary of her father's life since his hospitalization: "Now his life is back together. . . ." Caring about Wendy as a writer, and increasingly about Wendy herself, since she had begun to open her life to our view, we wondered about her ending to this narrative: What is its genre? Fairy tale? Realistic fiction? Is there a happily-ever-after like the ones Wendy finds in the young-adult novels she is reading? What choices might Wendy have about the ways she narrates her life? Our shaping questions began in turn to shape our instructional plans within the dialogic curriculum that Wendy now was shaping with us.

Although the effectiveness of the global organization of her writing is not matched at the local level—an ability to control words, phrases, sentences, and groups of sentences—this piece of writing is a dramatic improvement over the four impromptu pieces Wendy composed during September and October. Wendy still composes occasional constructions like these: "Me and my father were never really close or nor was he close to my brother, Steve"; "I never moved in with him, but I was scared to"; "Now his life is back together & even though he doesn't have my mom, but he does have a son and daughter who loves him very much." More frequently, however, she composes constructions like these: "When I was older, because of the situation at my house I wanted to go and live with my father, but I wasn't sure if I wanted to live with an alcoholic"; "When he was better, we took him out of St. Lukes' and transfered him to community Hospital, hoping that if he was in a alcoholism center he would stop drinking."

Until she undertook these assignments that required revising, and until we were persuaded that she wished to communicate with her readers, we had not discussed with Wendy her errors in usage (e.g., her opening construction *me and my brother*) or mechanics (e.g., her use of quotation marks in . . . *"I say to myself" He was the smart one*). Now, when she seemed engaged and had ample opportunities to revise her work before submitting it to us, we included discussions of usage and mechanics in our writing conferences. But these discussions—not surprisingly, given the openings she had offered us—always followed discussions of the meaning she was making for herself and for us with her writing. They always followed discussions of the discoveries she was making in and with her texts and the ways she was finding and using language to achieve such insight and balance as she could to relate the facts of her life to one another. Taking our lead from openings she provided, at this point our primary instructional goals for Wendy were to continue to help her explore the relationships that obtained between and among the ideas she was expressing in her writing and to focus her attention on how the authors of the young-adult novels she chose to read were giving literary shape to the themes and events that concerned her.

During December and January, when she turned to write again about a subject and theme that she had written about earlier, family traveling (W-4), Wendy did not compose a travel log, but a story that focuses on what she and her companions did during a family camping trip; relationships, their complexities, their implications, preoccupy her at this stage in her development:

W-6
Going Up North

When I was little, about 4 or 5. My family and I went up North a lot. We belonged to a camping club called Timbertowns Travelers. (Thats what they called Saginaw back then.) We would go camping almost every weekend during the summer time. Their were about 10 families in the group all together. We had a great time when we went up North. we would have potluck dinners & go trick or treating to all the trailers on Halloween.

I rember one cold day in August, we had gone to Tawas City to go camping with our club. We had past a lot of frozen ponds on the way up there. Their was our family and the Martin's who would kind of like hang with each other.

The Martin's had 1 boy Mike and 2 girls, Rhonda and Kim. After we got settled down, me and my brother Steve went over to get Mike, Rhonda, and Kim so we could go and get some thing to eat. We had left their trailer and didn't want to walk to get to the gate, so we decided to jump the fence to go to the A & W resternaut.

When we walked in, everybody just started to stare at us. we couldn't figure out why, so we kept on walking until we found an empty booth. After the waitress had taken our ordered, it was just 10 minutes before our food had arrived. After we got finished eating, Rhonda told me to put an A & W rootbeer mug under my hat. When I asked her why, "she said, She wanted to take home." I told her that I wasn't gonna do it, because I didn't want to get busted. She said that I wouldn't. I told her that something was wrong with her brain. I thought that the cold had something to do with it, but I finally gave in. I thought maybe something was wrong with my brain for stealing a mug. I qucikly put it under my hat & we left very swiftly & quickly. Then, as soon as we were out the door, I found myself running with a mug in my hand.

As soon as we got to the fence, we had to jump it to get back to the trailer park.

We went into our trailer and quickly shut the door. We all sat down and started to laugh, because we didn't get caught. After we had stopped laughing, we decided to play a fast game called Spoons. After we had played for a while, Mike was getting bored and decided to go ice fishing over to the pond.

When he was walking out the door, my brother Steve decided to go with him. So the both of left and Kim, Rhonda, and I decided to go sneak up of on them. We hurried & started following them. When Mike & Steve got to the pond, Mike was the 1st one on the ice. We were hidding by the bushes when we knew Mike had fallen into the water. We ran from the bushes where Steve was and him and Kim went to go get him but half way out there, Mike was standing in the middle of the pond drenched. He said the water only came up to his knees. We just suddenly bursted out laughing. They helped him out of the water and we hurried up to get back to the trailer so Mike could change.

We all took an oath saying we would never tell our parents, because they would kill us. Till this day, the still have no idea what all had happen that weekend, and probaby never will. When we look back, we will remember the great times we had with the Timbertown Camping Club.

In this piece, for the first time, Wendy tries to compose sustained dramatic action. In paragraphs four and seven, she writes longer chunks of discourse than she has tried before. Within each she describes the scene and actions of an adventure she, her brother, and their friends create when they are camping with their parents one cold day in Tawas City. As she experiments with new possibilities in her prose, Wendy writes energetically: "I quickly put it under my hat & left very swiftly & quickly"; "Mike was standing in the middle of the pond drenched." Rather than reporting talk indirectly as she did in W-5, Wendy uses talk both to provide her readers images of speaking persons and to lend her story the vitality of a drama. Furthermore, she creates her drama novelistically, coloring the events as Bruner (1986) tells us mature narrators do—by "subjectivizing" them, by depicting them "not through an omniscient eye that views a timeless reality, but through the filter of the consciousness of the protagonists in the story" (p. 25):

I told her that something was wrong with her brain. I thought that the cold had something to do with it, but I finally gave in. I thought maybe something was wrong with my brain for stealing a mug.

And, as in mature narratives, subjectivity—ways of looking toward a reality that must be constituted—is constituted of multiple perspectives: There is Rhonda's view, there is Wendy's; there are, though not stated, the views of parents, of local residents, of police—all of whom would see the theft as an event of a different kind. Wendy's understated opening, used to set a context for the event she will narrate, invites readers to think their own thoughts about perspectives, to imagine themselves in similar situations: "When we walked in, everybody just started to stare at us. We couldn't figure out why, so we kept on walking until we found an empty booth."

Reading these words in retrospect, thinking about perspectives, Wendy's narrative about theft becomes another kind of event. Did Wendy see that? We thought so. In an early move in the composition, Wendy reaches out to an audience imagined as distant from her, to readers who will need guidance to enter a personal world and its immediate constituents: "We belonged to a camping club called Timbertown Travelers. (That's what they called Saginaw back then.)". She prefigures a central event in her narrative in offering early a temporal reference and a detail about the landscape: "I remember one cold day in August, we had gone to Tawas City to go camping with our club. We had past a lot of frozen ponds on the way up there." Her more vivid depiction of action, her use of words to represent speaking persons, fits into this landscape. Wendy is more vividly remembering and imagining her world; furthermore, she is giving it texture in a way that will help her readers imagine it and remember events of their own making in similar worlds.

At this point in our course, we kept school. In a mid-year examination in which students composed a series of essays, we sought to learn how far our students had come by testing them in a situation that fits most schoolkeepers' notions of what a test—a writing assessment—should look like. We asked students to write three impromptu essays about teenage stress, each essay composed on a different day. On the fourth day, they were to revise one of the three essays or compose a fourth on the same subject.

Although Wendy told us in her evaluation of our mid-term exam that she "hated" the experience "because I don't have a lot of stories to write about plus I hate writing for that long a period," the essays she produced seemed to contradict her words. In reading them—and rereading them—we understood, though, that they must have been painful to compose. Wendy chose to elaborate on two themes she had been writing about since September: her relationships with her family and her relationships with her peers. In her first two impromptu writings (W-7 and W-8), Wendy wrote about her relationships with her family, more specifically, about her relationship with her mother. She chose to revise her third piece of impromptu writing, an essay about her relationships with her peers, on the fourth day of the examination (W-9).

When we compared these three with the four impromptu essays Wendy composed in September, we saw her growth as a writer, her improvement in global organization, local control, usage, and the mechanics of writing. But we found still more impressive Wendy's continuing exploration of the themes that defined the focus of her intellectual project. "The Most Stressful Situation That I Have Had" (W-7), "Throwing Snowballs From the Roof" (W-8), and "My Friends" (W-9) constitute an obvious invitation, in their themes, situations, and characters, to intertextual readings. We read W-9 as a rereading, on our part and Wendy's, of "Unrest at Home" (W-4) and "My Father" (W-5); and we read it as the introduction to another text that Wendy composed in W-7, W-8, and W-9.

From W-7
[The Most Stressful Situation That I Have Had]

> The most stressful situation that I have had is when my parents were divorced while I was in the 6th grade. As soon as they were divorced my mother's friend and her two kids moved in with my mom & my brother Steve. It was reallyhard on me and Steve because we wanted our dad to come back to live with us. . . . And I just think, and then I start to cry. I try not to, but it gets me mad because I think my life is worth nothing.

Reading W-7 as the third in the series W-4, W-5, and W-7, we saw Wendy reopen her investigation of her relationship to her parents; reading it as the first in the series W-7, W-8, and W-9, we saw Wendy reopening her investigation to explore her relationship with her mother. We saw something else as well: signs that Wendy was developing a research method for inquiring into the issues she was studying. In "Unrest at Home" (W-4), after rehearsing the difficulties she had relating to her mother, her mother's friend, and that friend's children, Wendy asserted that she "wanted to live at [her] dads anyway." However, in "My Father" (W-5), after accounting for her parents' divorce, Wendy described an especially painful weekend she spent with her dad, and, in so doing, she made problematic the assertion she had made in W-4. Moving from an assertion about the relationship she wished to have with her dad to a description that caused her to question that assertion, Wendy created a crisis in her life with her father, one that required resolution. In W-5, she wrote that her father's drinking "became so bad, that my mom and her friend took my dad into the hospital . . ." where he received treatment for his alcoholism. Having composed a crisis and laid the groundwork for its resolution, Wendy inscribed her reconciliation with her father in "the first conversation we evr had," a conversation in which she told him "how proud I was for him to stop drinking."

In W-7, W-8, and W-9, following the same research method she used to explore her relationship to her father, Wendy makes claims about her relationship with her mother, problematizes those claims, and frames them into a problem that demands resolution; but she inscribes no resolution to the problem she has framed.[8] In "The Most Stressful Situation That I Have Had" (W-7), Wendy reopens the text she began in "Unrest at Home" (W-4), supplying her readers more information about the reconfiguration of relationships in her home that occurred when she was in 6th grade. In "Throwing Snowballs From the Roof" (W-8), instead of describing a crisis in her relationship with her mother, Wendy's developing stylistic awareness of her self as a "creative writer" leads her to dramatize the confrontation:

W-8
[Throwing Snowballs From the Roof]

It was in the winter of '86. There was snow on the ground and very cold. me & my friends Tammie & Kurt were over to my house. we were throwing snowballs at cars. All Just out of the blue Kurt asked if we wanted to go up on the roof to throw snowballs. I asked him. What's the hell with you. If I ever was to get caught up there, my mom would kick my ass.

Tammi and Kurt started to call me a chicken Shit. So I got pissed off and we climbed on top of the roof. I was really scared because I was scared to death about heights. We were up there for about 1/2 hour, throwing snowballs at cars. then we jumped down because Tammie & Kurt had to go home.

So I was in the living watching TV when she my mom came home. She was in a pissy ass mood because she was fed up with her job. The next thing I knew. The next door neighbor had told [my mom's friend] I was up on the roof and she told my mom. When my mom found out, she went crazy, she started to really bitch me out for being up there. I told her that there was nothing wrong to having some fun. The next thing I knew she started bitching even more. When I looked up to say something, she threw a coffee cup, filled with coffee at the door. The cup shattered into pieces.

I just sat their, then she told me I was grounded for a week and I couldn't have my 16th birthday party. Then she ran out the door. I was never so shocked before in my life. I had never see her act the way she did, but know I understand about all the pressure she was going through.

In W-8, Wendy explicitly expresses her anger toward her mother, anger she suggested in W-7 ("It was reallyhard on me and Steve because we wanted our dad to come back to live with us"; "I hated the whole situation"; "And I just think, and then I start to cry. I try not to, but it gets me mad because I think my life is worth nothing."). With uncharacteristic irony, however, in the first two paragraphs of W-8, Wendy composes a situation that prepares her readers to understand her anger toward her mother as misplaced anger. Not only does she indicate that she is aware that her actions will displease her mother, but she also indicates that she herself is frightened by what she is doing:

All Just out of the blue Kurt asked if we wanted to go up on the roof to throw snowballs. I asked him. What's the hell with you. If I ever was to get caught up there, my mom would kick my ass.

Tammi and Kurt started to call me a chicken Shit. So I got pissed off and we climbed on top of the roof. I was really scared because I was scared to death about heights.

In spite of disobeying her mother's expectations and frightening herself in doing so, Wendy chooses to be indignant when her mother chastises her for misbehaving:

When my mom found out, she went crazy, she started to really bitch me out for being up there. I told her that there was nothing wrong to having some fun. The next thing I knew she started bitching even more. When I looked up to say something, she threw a coffee cup, filled with coffee at the door. The cup shattered into pieces

Earlier in the year, we recognized several of Wendy's underwritten narrative-essays as curricular invitations she was composing for herself, invitations calling for elaboration and clarification of problems she was working to define. At this time, we recognized that the dramatic crises she was composing into her narrative-essays were functioning to translate those elaborated and clarified problems into questions that required answers within Wendy's developing intellectual project. In "My Father" (W-5), for example, we believe Wendy posed these questions: How can I relate to my father? How shall I relate to him? And we believe she answered them in this fashion: I can relate to my father after he undergoes treatment for his illness. I shall relate to him by loving him. We suspected that Wendy may well have learned this composing strategy for shaping and solving problems from the young-adult novels she was reading in which action was consistently plotted to rise, climax, fall, and be resolved.

As the students of her texts that we were becoming, we read "My Friends" (W-9), juxtaposed as it is to "Throwing Snowballs from the Roof" (W-8), as a move on Wendy's part to compose a more realistic resolution to the tension that existed between her and her mother than the formulaic one she had been reading in young-adult novels and that she had previously been composing herself.

W-9
[My Friends]

There are days when I think to myself, where did I meet my friends at. Most of my friends that I hang around with is involved in smoking pot, taking speeders and some other kinds of drugs.

I'm the only one out of my friends who has never did any kind of drug before in my life. The only think I have ever tried is drinking, but I only drink once in a great while. I don't drink beer and all the hard stuff, I drink California Coolers.

Most of the time they try to get me to get high or drunk with them. I really don't hang around with them too much anymore because I am always working, so I guess I use for an excuse.

My best friend Tammie, who has a brain tumor always want to go out and party. She gets high and drunk all the time. I don't know why she does it, maybe so everybody will thinks she's cool, but drinking and getting high is not cool, it is plain stupid.

I thought maybe that by Tammie mixing drugs and alcohol, it ? may have an effect in on the tumor which is lodged in her brain.

While I'm around her & some other friends while they are high, it seems we can communicate a lot better, but while they are straight, all they are concerned about is getting more drugs in the body. I have a problem with being with them while they are high because they want to get into rouble. I mean I have fun with them, but then they get to the point where they want more excitment, so it's hard on me. I usually just tell ? them I have to go home or go to work. Usually my excuses work. All my friends, well most of them any way always ask me why I haven't ever tried drugs. I would just tell them that I can have a great time, just like any other person who is on drugs. The only thing is, is that I am not and never will be for the rest of my life.

Peer pressure is very stressful to a teenager. It has many effects on us, but in many different ways. Your peers may say "if you don't do this or that" it will be the end of a very good relationship between you and your friends. Its hard on me because they think I a I am a total square because I ??t don't do drugs or alcohol. I don't skip school and I get pretty good marks in school. They don't understand what it is like for me. All they are concerned about is getting involve in drugs. They don't even try to understand, and I just wish they would.

In "My Friends" (W-9), Wendy reflects on her disappointment in her peers in terms that invite her readers to understand the piece, in part, as commentary on W-8. In W-8, when Kurt and Tammie pressure her to join them in throwing snowballs from the roof, Wendy's first reaction to the suggestion is concern about her mother's disapproval. Only secondarily is she concerned about her well-being. Her participation in her friends' scheme earns her what she had anticipated: her mothers's anger. It does not cause her harm. When she writes about the excuses she has developed to avoid getting involved in the "excitement" her friends have continued to propose to her, excitement that carries with it most worrisome consequences, Wendy demonstrates that her mother's concern for her well-being has become her own:

> I have a problem with being with them while they are high because they want to get into trouble. I mean I have fun with them, but then they get to the point where they want more excitment, so it's hard on me. I usually just tell them I have to go home or go to work. Usually my excuses work. All my friends, well most of them any way always ask me why I haven't ever tried drugs. I would just tell them that I can have a great time, just like any other person who is on drugs. The only thing is, is that I am not and never will be for the rest of my life.

W-9 offers a significant shift in Wendy's textual persona. She is not the child angry with her parent for disappointments her parent cannot remedy for her; she is not the child angry with her parent because she wants to break her parent's rules; she is a young woman shaping values and a life style within the circumstances in which she finds herself. The conclusions she composes to W-8 and W-9 bespeak Wendy's shifting perspective. She concludes W-8 with an observation about her mother: "I understand about all the pressure she was going through"; she concludes W-9 with an observation about her friends: "They don't even try to understand, and I just wish they would."

In W-7, W-8, and W-9, the three writings she composed for the mid-year examination, Wendy has written her way from childish anger toward mature understanding. Having offered herself an opportunity to resolve her tension with her mother, as she resolved her tension with her father, by composing a crisis in their relationship, Wendy takes up her self-composed opportunity differently than she did when she wrote about her father (W-5) and shaped a happily-ever-after resolution to his problems and to her relationship with him:

> Ever since he got out of the Hospital, he hasn't touched a drop of alcohol. It has been about a year since he drank. Now all he drinks is pop & coffee. I am so happy that he quit. Now his life is back together & even though he doesn't have my mom, but he does have a son and daughter who loves him very much.

In the trilogy formed by W-7, W-8, and W-9, Wendy composes a different kind of resolution. She does not indicate that she feels comfortable or easy with her mother, as she suggests she came to feel with her father; rather, Wendy explains that she understands her mother is experiencing unusual pressure. One reading of her understanding is, of course, that the tension between them is her mother's problem and not Wendy's, or not theirs in common. Yet in W-9, Wendy makes a move of another kind—one she has learned to make in her development as a writer. Although she does not explicitly acknowledge that she may, in part, be responsible for arguments between herself and her mother, she positions herself as an actor in a dramatically realized situation where her friends' values play out against her mother's. Wendy does not say that her mother's indignation was right; she does not claim, as she did with her father, that she loves her mother "very much." Rather, she aligns herself with her mother's values as one who would compose another kind of life from that of her friends. Her statement is implicit, not explicit. Wendy does not say there was some righteousness in her mother's indignation; she does not promise that life is "back together." Her fairy-tale endings are gone, unreplaced at this point in her research project.

In February, students shifted their focus from collecting and composing growing-up stories to critiquing and analyzing those stories in the light of the literature they had been reading. In preparation for composing and publishing an anthology of their writings, students read a collection of seven pieces of one another's writing. In small groups and as a class, they became fully familiar with the range of themes and literary styles that characterized their growing-up experiences and stories, and they advised one another about which pieces were most successful and why.

Wendy chose to develop "Going Up North" (W-6) for publication. In her essay, she chose to write about the good times she and her family had together when they were traveling:

W-10
Camping in Tawas City

When I was little, about four or five, my family and I went up north a lot. We belonged to a camping club called the "Timbertown Travelers." Timbertown is what people called Saginaw back then. We would go camping almost every weekend during the summertime. There were about ten families in the group all together. We had a great time when we went up north. We would have potluck dinners and go trick or treating to all of the trailers on Halloween.

I remember one cold day in January, when we went to Tawas City on a camping trip. Our family and the Martin family hung out with each other. The Martins had a boy, Mike, and two girls, Rhonda and Kim. After we got settled down, my brother Steve and I went over to get Mike, Rhonda, and Kim, so that we could all go and get something to eat. We left their trailer and, because it was a long walk, we decided to jump the fence to go to the A&W restaurant. When we walked in, everybody in the restaurant just stared at us. We couldn't figure out why, so we kept on walking until we found an empty booth to sit down. After we finished eating, Rhonda leaned over to me and said, "Put that mug under your hat."

I said, "Are you nuts? I'm not gonna get caught stealing a mug."

"Oh, come on, she whined. "You're not gonna get caught. Who'll know?"

"Well, if you want it that bad, you steal it."

"No, sause I don't have a hat and you do. Besides, they will get suspicious if I wear your hat."

"O.k., but if I get caught, it's your fault."

I thought maybe something was wrong with my brain for stealing a stupid mug worth pennies. I quickly put the mug under my hat, and we left very swiftly and sneakily. Then, as soon as we were out the door, I found myself running with the mug in my hand. When we got to the trailer entrance, we had to jump the fence to get back into the trailer park.

We went back into the trailer and quickly shut the door. We all sat down and started to laugh, because we didn't get caught. After we stopped laughing, we decided to play a fast game called "Spoons". After we played for a while, Mike got bored and decided to go ice fishing at a pond outside of the park. When Mike walked out the door, my brother Steve decided to go with him. After they both left, and Kim, Rhonda, and I decided to sneak up on them.

When Mike and Steve got to the pond, Mike was the first one on the ice. We were hiding by the bushes when we heard something. The next thing we knew, Mike had fallen into the water. We ran from the bushes where Steve was watching him. When we got to the edge of the pond, Kim tried a rescue attempt on Mike, but when she started to make the attempt to rescue him, Mike just stood up in the middle of the pond, drenched with icy water. He said that the water only came to his knees. We burst out laughing. We all helped Mike out of the water and then hurried up to get back to the trailer so Mike could change his clothes.

We all took an oath, vowing we would never tell our parents, because they would kill us for not telling them what had all happened that weekend in Tawas City. But I'm hoping when they read this story they will forgive us. When we look back, we will remember the great times we had with the Timbertown Travelers' Club.

We read in "Camping in Tawas City" (W-10) several things we were not surprised to find in the light of Wendy's developing work. We read a text in which Wendy refines the first sustained dramatic action she composed. She chooses to heighten the drama of the restaurant scene by replacing indirect speech with the direct dialogue which she has mastered the conventions for composing. She revises this passage in W-6:

> .... After we got finished eating, Rhonda told me to put an A & W rootbeer mug under my hat. When I asked her why, "she said, She wanted to take home." I told her that I wasn't gonna do it, because I didn't want to get busted. She said that I wouldn't. I told her that something was wrong with her brain. I thought that the cold had something to do with it, but I finally gave in.

into this passage in W-10:

> After we finished eating, Rhonda leaned over to me and said, "Put that mug under your hat."
>
> I said, "Are you nuts? I'm not gonna get caught stealing a mug."
>
> "Oh, come on, she whined. "You're not gonna get caught. Who'll know?"
>
> "Well, if you want it that bad, you steal it."
>
> "No, cause I don't have a hat and you do. Besides, they will get suspicious if I wear your hat."
>
> "O.k., but if I get caught, it's your fault."
>
> I thought maybe something was wrong with my brain for stealing a stupid mug worth pennies.

In her revision, Wendy has made other small but significant changes. In the W-6 version, she is the pawn in Rhonda's plan. Wendy writes: "I told her there was something wrong with her brain." But in W-10, Wendy recognizes herself as the actor in the scene: "I thought maybe something was wrong with my brain for stealing a stupid mug worth pennies." In this small but significant revision, Wendy indicates an understanding that she is responsible for her actions, that her life is not determined simply by the actions of others. Wendy concluded W-6 with this passage:

> We all took an oath saying we would never tell our parents, because they would kill us. Till this day, the still have no idea what all had happen that weekend, and probaby never will. When we look back, we will remember the great times we had with the Timbertown Camping Club.

She revised that conclusion in W-10 to read this way:

> We all took an oath, vowing we would never tell our parents, because they would kill us for not telling them what had all happened that weekend in Tawas City. But I'm hoping when they read this story they will forgive us. When we look back, we will remember the great times we had with the Timbertown Travelers' Club.

When she wrote W-6, Wendy had moved herself and her parents back to earlier, happier times for them, and it was those times that she chose to inscribe and publish in *The Bridge*. But in W-10 she does not choose to leave her family in earlier times before their troubles. She moves them into a time after those troubles, a time when she can acknowledge her humanity and ask her parents to recognize it, a time in which perhaps she can acknowledge her parents' humanity.

The writings she composed during the academic year and the one she developed for *The Bridge* with editorial advice from her classmates and her teachers constitute full and rich evidence for us to conclude that the work she did with reading and writing during the 1987-88 academic year should earn Wendy high marks in any evaluator's book. But we knew that others might wish another kind of evidence of her writing competencies: a sample or samples of Wendy's untutored writing. For this reason, we asked Wendy and her classmates to write for two days at the end of May about the Montague Inn, a gracious bed-and-breakfast in Saginaw. We saw this writing task not only as an occasion for a final examination but also as an opportunity to finish some unfinished business. In late March, we had visited the Inn on a field trip. Because we were working to publish *The Bridge*, we had not discussed the Inn and our trip to it as fully as we wished we had.[9] For their final examination, we invited Wendy and her classmates to refer to their memories of their visit to the Inn, the notes they had taken during that visit, and the pieces of writing they had read about it in order to prepare themselves to write about the Inn during two class sessions. We encouraged students to draft an essay on the first day of the exam and revise it on the second day. At the beginning of the first day, Wendy composed W-11; mid-way through the 55-minute class period, she put it aside and composed W-12.

Given the kind of writings they were—composed within the constraints of a 55-minute class period—and the time when they were written—at the end of our course of study together—we could not help but compare the hastily composed W-11 and W-12 with Wendy's first writings. Peppered with the mechanical and usage errors that characterize her unrevised writing, the compositions Wendy composed for her final exam in May not only serve as a picture of the quality of her untutored writing at the time, but they also serve as a picture of the workings of the curriculum of *Inquiry and Expression*. In W-11 and W-12, Wendy creates an occasion that enables her to fulfill her teachers' plans for her to write about the Montague Inn and to pursue her own project of composing the relationships between and among the members of her family. Circling back to her earlier texts, she gathers the characters that matter to her—her mother, her father, her brother Steve, and his fiance Dawn:

From W-11

It's 9:00 a.m. Saturday morning and my mother, Dawn, and I were getting ready for Dawn and Steve's wedding. We were in our bedroom in the Montague Inn waiting until 1:00 p.m. when the wedding is supposed to start.

From W-12

Well after I had graduated we (my mother, Dawn and I) spent the night there to get ready for the wedding. Steve and my dad stayed in the room next door.

And she brings them to the Montague Inn, which she describes in some detail both to create a setting for the wedding and to satisfy her teachers' plan that she write about the Inn in this final exam:

From W-12

I told him that I found out that a couple named Mr. and Mrs. Kinney bought the house and remodeled it. It became a beautiful home with plenty of rooms where people can stay. The Montague Inn is one of a kind. Friends of the Kinney's had helped out in the remodeling and had plenty of fun. I told Steve I also found out that the Inn was a very popular place because of its nice faculties and the way they treat you like one of the family.

Every thing was going along great. I was now getting closer to 1:00 and everybody was getting nervous. I went walking around and I noticed that there were a lot of bedroom and even a kitchen downstairs. I was so amused that I just kept walking around admiring all the beautiful things. I even lost track of time. When I finally noticed what time it was I only had 10 minutes until the wedding started. I ran to the bedroom and got dressed. Then it was time. We went out to the Herb Garden where everything was set up beautifully.

Characters gathered, setting described, Wendy stages a fairy-tale wedding, like the ones she has read about in the young-adult novels, like the ones she has composed herself:

From W-12

Then it was time. We went out to the Herb Garden where everything was set up beautifully. Then the wedding bells began to ring. The wedding was starting. I couldn't believe it. I was actually getting a sister-in-law. Then it happened! They were married. I was so happy. Now that the wedding was over, now I could look forward to the reception. That was held in the hall. It was a great reception. There was dancing and music and everybody was having a great time. Then Steve and Dawn left for there honeymoon in Hawaii. Steve and Dawn were married June 11, 1988 at the Montague Inn. Now they live in Jacksonville, Florida with one son Steve Jr. and one daughter named Lisa.

Although we encouraged students to revise the compositions they had written the previous day, on the second day of their final examination Wendy chose not to do that. She completely abandoned the work she had begun in W-11 and W-12, electing instead to leave behind her the fairy tale she had been composing. In W-13, a piece we described as realistic fiction, Wendy wrote her final composition for *Inquiry and Expression*.

W-13
The Montague Inn

I remember growing up in Florida with my mother in a small apartment with only one bedroom and one bathroom and the dining room connected with each other. I would always dream about living in a huge house, having at least ten bedrooms and at least four bathrooms. I knew that someday I would either be able to live in a house that big or I could one day see the inside of one. I remember the day my mother told me we were going to visit my mother's sister in Saginaw, Michigan. I was so excited, I wanted to leave right away. My mother told me we were leaving the next day, so I hurried up and packed everything that I could. When we got to the Detroit Metropolitan Airport, my mother's sister Pat was waiting for us to get off the plane. When we were in the airport we saw my Aunt Pat waiting for us. I just dropped my bags and ran over to her to give her a big hug. On the way home my Aunt Pat told us what she had in mind for us to do while we stayed with Aunt Pat and her family. She said the most exciting thing to do is to see the Montague Inn. I had asked her what it was and she told me that it was an old house where people from anywhere could stay the night. My Aunt Pat told my mother and I that the home had about 15 bedrooms. I was so excited that I could finally see a beautiful home like that I asked her when we could go see it and she did the following day because we had to go back to her house so we could rest and get something to eat.

After we had something to eat I went to bed because I thought that the night would go faster. But it took me a while to fall alseep because I was so excited. Then the day came to visit the Montague Inn. When we got there I was astonished at such a wonderful home it was. I couldn't imagine anything bigger. When we walked in the doors I could feel a chill running up my spine. Mr. and Mrs. Kinney gave us a tour of the home and told us how her and her husband and friends did most of the remodeling themselves. They told us about Mr. Montague and his two children. They showed us all the bedrooms and the outside by the herb garden. It was great. After the tour was over Mr. and Mrs. Kinney told us how nice of a pleasure it was to show us around. We thanked her and as we were going out the door my Aunt Pat remembered that she had locked her keys in her car. So my Aunt had to call her house and have her son Todd bring out an extra pair. While we waited, Mr. and Mrs. Kinney asked us to stay for lunch. So we did. The lunch was really too fancy for me though, I just assume stick with my 2 favorites Old Town Drive Inn and Macdonald's. Todd had arrived just as we finished eating. We thanked her again and left. When my mother and I left for Florida I said to myself that someday I would start a Montague Inn where I live.

In fulfillment of our plans and her project, Wendy writes about the Montague Inn and her family. And she does something else: she seems to issue another curricular invitation to herself. With W-13, she appears to have concluded the text she was writing during the 1987–88 academic year and to have introduced a new one, one that does not focus on the past, one that looks to the future.

I smiled when I first read this last piece of writing Wendy composed for the course we had constructed together, and I smile again as I read it now. Perhaps I do so because she begins the piece by placing herself in Florida, a place I know she likes because she told me so in one of the earliest texts she composed for our course (W-3). Perhaps I'm smiling because because I enjoy the way she moves herself from Florida to the Montague Inn, which she has to write about to fulfill her teachers' plans for this assignment; or because she mentions my friends, Kathryn and Norman Kinney, innkeepers of the Montague Inn, my home away from home when I was in Saginaw. Perhaps I'm smiling because she writes about misplaced the keys to her father's car, and that detail makes me remember that Wendy misplaced her car keys the day our class visited the Montague Inn; or perhaps because Wendy leaves the Inn to take a journey with her mother, and I am a mother. Perhaps I smile for some combination of these reasons; perhaps for all of them. I know I smile because the text makes connections with me and for me.

As a demonstration of what she learned from the research she conducted in the *Inquiry and Expression* course, W-13 is not only about the connections Wendy is able to make with and for one of the teacher-readers, it is also quite obviously about the connections she has made between and among the concerns she addressed in her intellectual project in the course, connections she has made with and for herself. Wendy's act of literate composition in W-13, what James Boyd White would call an act of "intellectual integration,"[10] represents the kind of literacy the *Inquiry and Expression* course invited students to develop. As such, it illustrates the ways in which our students engaged in complex acts of reading and writing in order to compose and recompose their lived experiences in the light of their developing understandings, and it testifies to the learning—to the expanded perspectives—that reading and writing make possible for all of us who engage in those activities for the purpose of making significant personal and communal meanings.

Wendy's act of literate composition in W-13 also illustrates why we teacher-evaluators believe that descriptions of students' writing competencies must be especially shaped for the particular audiences who have a vested interest in those students and their writing. Just as we teacher-evaluators offered different evidence of their developing literacy to students themselves, to our professional colleagues, and to members of the communities in which we and our students live and work, in support of my conviction that "The Montague Inn" demonstrates Wendy Gunlock's ability to compose complex meanings for herself and for her communities, I would shape my claim and the evidence I would offer in support of that claim differently for Wendy, for my professional colleagues, and for the members of the various communities in which Wendy lives. For example, in an informal conversation with Wendy, I would make comments like these to let her know how much I appreciate her and her work: "You are clever. You got those keys in that essay." And I would ask questions like these to indicate my respect for her work and to support her continuing development as a writer: "Why did you begin the piece in Florida? Where did Aunt Pat come from? Does she live in Florida? How does she figure in your text?" In an essay such as this one, I would draw my professional colleagues' attention to how complicated a business it is to account for Wendy's literacy learning and how such an account is always and only particular interpretations by particular individuals who read meanings into what they construe to be evidence of that learning. In a meeting of the Board of Education in Saginaw, I would invite public-minded citizens to read the piece Wendy wrote about the Montague Inn in one class hour, under examination circumstances, and I would propose that students in the schools might serve the community's needs as they learn to read and write by composing and publishing a booklet for the Chamber of Commerce about local points of interest to teenagers, just as those students had served the community when they composed and published *The Bridge*. My point in shaping these different statements about the quality of a student's writing, like the argument of this essay, is this: Even as reading and writing are complex human activities that take place within complex human relationships, meaningful descriptions of particular acts of reading and writing are themselves complex human activities that take place within complex human relationships. If they are to serve, courses in schools must invite students to engage themselves fully in complexly situated acts of reading and writing, and those of us who take upon ourselves the task of accounting for that engagement must do so in equally complexly situated texts.

Notes

[1] I co-taught with Jane Denton and Sharon Floyd, high school English teachers in Saginaw, Michigan, one 12th grade English class in each of Saginaw's two comprehensive high schools. Jay L. Robinson, Professor of English and Director of the Center for Educational Improvement through Collaboration (CEIC) at the University of Michigan, joined us in our planning and frequently in our classes so that he might be a fully participating observer of our work. At that time, I was a Lecturer in the Department of English and Coordinator of Research Projects for the CEIC.

Although this essay represents my understanding of the work we did together, that understanding is so deeply informed by my colleagues that the work I write about must be understood as ours. For her contributions to my thinking, I am also indebted to Wendy Gunlock; she is now a part-time student at Delta Community College, University Center, Michigan. During the 1987-88 academic year she was a student at Arthur Hill High

School in Saginaw, a middle-sized industrial city whose public schools serve a multi-ethnic community: 53% of Saginaw's students are black, 32% white, 13% Hispanic.

The work described here was sponsored by the CEIC, the Office of the Vice President for Minority Affairs at the University of Michigan, the W. K. Kellogg Foundation, and the School District of the City of Saginaw.

[2]In his important book, *Horace's Compromise*, Theodore Sizer (1984) makes a persuasive argument that secondary English studies in the United States should be reconceived as studies in inquiry and expression.

[3]For a full discussion of the ways in which teachers' instructional plans and students' intellectual projects interanimate one another to construct curriculum, see Patricia Lambert Stock, *The Dialogic Curriculum: Teachers and Students Researching Together* (Portsmouth, N.H.: Boynton/Cook Heinemann, forthcoming). In *The Dialogic Curriculum*, I present an interpretative case study of Wendy Gunlock's writing for *Inquiry and Expression*—including the compositions discussed here—as evidence for my claims that unless and until teachers' plans are engaged by students they remain just that—plans.

[4]Because many of our students were parents of infant children, because almost all held full-time jobs outside of school, because some were both parents and workers, we promised that they would be able to do the required work during class. Many students elected to do work outside class; in fact, a majority came to school on Saturdays in the spring when we were working to publish their research.

[5]*The Bridge* is available for $7.50 a copy from CEIC, 2018 School of Education Building, University of Michigan, Ann Arbor, MI 48109.

> One of the peculiarities of composition research's treatment of student writing has been that, despite an otherwise voracious methodological eclecticism, it has never adopted any hermeneutical method: that is, a method wherein the primary concern is to interpret the writing of individual students as meaningful, communicative discourse (p. 28).

[6]In planning for and publishing their anthology, students helped us test the viability of offering communities evidence of students' literacy other than numerical summaries. This evidence was well received in the local community and beyond. Publication of *The Bridge*, which was sponsored by the CEIC and the School District of the City of Saginaw, was treated as an event in Saginaw. The student-authors introduced the book to the community at a book-signing party at the Montague Inn in Saginaw in June 1987. The event was covered by local newspaper, radio, and television stations. A year and a half later, in October 1989, a well-received, favorably reviewed adaptation of *The Bridge* was produced in Saginaw by students from the school district's Center for Arts and Sciences.

The book has been purchased and read by hundreds of people beyond the local community. It is required reading in Sylvia Robin's *Introductory Composition* course at Delta Community College, University Center, Michigan; in Marian Mohr and Marian MacLean's course *The Teacher as Researcher* at George Mason University, Fairfax, Virginia; in Loren Barritt's course in the *Psychology of Education* at the University of Michigan; and in Marni Schwartz's classes at Niskayuna Middle School in Schenectady, New York.

[7]For ease of reference, when Wendy has not titled her compositions, we have. We distinguish between her titles and ours by enclosing ours in brackets.

[8]I believe that the way we conducted the mid-year examination may have had something to do with Wendy's decision to write about her relationship to her mother on this occasion. We teachers had decided to each tell a stressful story about our own teenage years to illustrate the kinds of stories students might write for their exams. At the

start of each of the four days of the exam, one of us told or read a story about ourselves, a narrative within which we intentionally reflected on the event or events we reported. Jane Denton told her story the first day of the exam in Wendy's class. It was a story that made her vulnerable to her students, students—like Wendy—who clearly respected her, students—like Wendy—who were clearly fond of her. Jane Denton's willingness to share and reflect on a sensitive problem she had had as a teenager invited our students to do the same.

[9]We had left the experience of visiting the Montague Inn largely unstudied. One day in class, we composed thank-you notes to Kathryn Kinney, one of the Inn's owners, who had given us a tour of the Inn and told us stories about the original owners of the house, and to members of the Inn's staff, who had described to us the renovations they had undertaken to convert the historic house into an Inn and the nature of their work to operate the Inn on a day-to-day basis. Another day in class, we read several pieces of writing about the Inn—a press release for its opening and compositions written by community college students who had also toured it.

[10]In his book *Justice as Translation*, James Boyd White (1990) argues that "what is called for in our life with language, and with one another, is an art of composition," which he describes as the capacity for "intellectual integration" (p. xiv). White explains what he means by "intellectual integration" in this way:

> What I mean by integration is a kind of composition, and then in a literal, and literary sense: a putting together of two things to make out of them a third, a new whole, with a meaning of its own. In this process the elements combined do not lose their identities but retain them, often in clarified form, yet each comes to mean something different as well, when it is seen in relation to the other. In this sense each element is transformed, as it becomes part of something else, an entity existing at a new level of complexity. At the same time we ourselves are transformed as well, both as makers of the new object in the world and as those who engage with it (p. 4).

References

Bruner, Jerome. (1986). *Actual Minds, Possible Worlds.* Cambridge, Mass.: Harvard University Press.

Gunlock, Wendy. (1987). "Camping Up North." *The Bridge.* Ann Arbor, Mich.: Center for Educational Improvement through Collaboration, pp. 36-38.

North, Stephen M. (October 1986). "Writing in a Philosophy Class." *Research in the Teaching of English* 20, 3: 225-262.

Sizer, Theodore. (1984). *Horace's Compromise.* Boston: Houghton Mifflin.

Stock, Patricia Lambert. (In press). *The Dialogic Curriculum: Students and Teachers Researching Together.* Portsmouth, N.H.: Boynton/Cook Heinemann.

Stock, Patricia Lambert. (1990). "Taking on Testing: Chapter Two," in *Hands-on Assessment of Elementary School Science,* edited by George E. Hein. Grand Forks, N.D.: North Dakota Study Group on Evaluation.

Stock, Patricia Lambert, and Jay L. Robinson. (1987). "Taking on Testing: Teachers as Tester-Researchers." *English Education* 19, 2: 93-121.

White, James Boyd. (1990). *Justice as Translation.* Chicago, Ill.: University of Chicago Press.

7

Active Assessment for Active Science

George E. Hein

The Need for Active Assessment Methods

Science is an active process that involves using physical skills, imagination, and creativity to tackle the usually ill-defined problems and events of the real world. In looking at our methods for assessing science learning in schools, however, we might think that what's most important in science is being able to choose the one correct answer for each question on a multiple-choice test. Assessing science through multiple-choice tests is like assessing Larry Bird's basketball skills by asking him to respond to a set of multiple-choice questions. We might find out something about Bird's knowledge of the facts of basketball, perhaps even something about his conceptual knowledge, but we certainly would not be able to measure the level of his playing skill.

Increasingly, commentators on the state of science education recognize this mismatch. The National Science Foundation (NSF) in 1987 launched a major curriculum development initiative that began with elementary school projects and will add middle school and high school projects in later years. In a memorandum on assessment written in the second year of this effort, a group of the NSF-supported curriculum developers concluded:

> Research shows that extant achievement tests do not measure the broad range of scientific processes or higher order thinking skills; nor do they give insight into naive versus "scientific" interpretations of phenomena. All these domains are integral to current approaches to teaching and learning science. . . . On the contrary, because the emphasis of these norm-referenced tests is on types of questions that can be answered by

Author's note: I am grateful for the support of the National Science Foundation, Grant #TPE-885032, which contributed to the collection of material for this chapter.

simple recall of facts, and/or recognition of textbook experiments, they militate against the less predictable hands-on approach. . . . The existing norm-referenced tests not only fail to support or encourage the implementations of new developments in science curriculum and pedagogy, but their continued, near-universal use may dampen or totally inhibit implementation of such approaches. Thus, there is a need for alternatives to existing national, normreferenced tests. The alternatives must be of high quality and must meet the public's needs for accountability and comparability across programs and districts. Additionally, they must be congruent with the philosophy of science teaching and learning the National Science Foundation promotes (Harmon et al. 1988).

The National Center for Improving Science Education, a policy group whose mission is "to promote changes in state and local policies and practices in the science curriculum, science teaching, and assessment of student learning in science" (Raizen et al. 1989), has begun to issue a series of reports covering assessment, curriculum, and teacher training at the elementary, middle, and secondary school levels. In the first report on assessment, the expert panel convened by the Center stresses the need for new and more varied assessment methods and argues for a national program to improve science assessment:

Improvement Goal 2. Development of externally mandated assessments as well as classroom tests that conform closely to the characteristics of good science curricula and instruction. . . . Assessments should provide greater opportunities for children to interact with stimulus materials, (2) attend to understandings of constructs and principles as well as factual knowledge, (3) probe approaches to problem solving as well as outcomes, (4) be explicitly integrated with the curriculum and with instruction, (5) incorporate hands-on activities whenever feasible, and (6) be structured around group as well as individual activities (Raizen et al. 1989, p. 97).

These are but two examples of calls for a reform, indeed a revolution, in how we assess knowledge of science. Every major policy paper of the past few years, whether focused on national indicators (Knapp et al. 1987, Murnane and Raizen 1988) or on classroom practice (Resnick 1987; Champagne, Lovitts, and Calinger 1990), has called for a similar change in assessment.

Fortunately, developing alternatives to multiple-choice assessments need not start de novo. As long as teachers have wondered about what students have learned, a wide range of assessment strategies and practices have flourished. The dominant use of paper-and-pencil tests at the national level has only obscured, not eliminated, the alternative work that has taken place in a variety of settings and at levels ranging from the classroom to national-scale assessments. Much recent work is well documented and relevant to any effort to develop classroom-based and large-scale alternative assessments.

In this chapter, I summarize a number of different ways by which learning in science has been and can be effectively assessed, and I describe a few cases in detail as illustrations of more widespread practice. I begin by outlining the various methods that are available to assess student learning in science. I next examine several categories of research and development used to look at learning in science, and discuss the methods professionals in these fields have employed. Finally, I discuss a few issues that emerge from this catalog of methods.

I do not cover a number of technical issues related to assessment. For example, all types of assessment are subject to questions concerning reliability and validity. In general, the simpler the method to administer and score, and the less the method is subject to variation because of local circumstances or context, the easier it is to establish reliability. However, the same conditions generally make the validity of the results more difficult to achieve, since the requirements for a simple, all-purpose test that can be administered in any context usually mean that the assessment differs from the actual activity that is being assessed. Thus, a paper-and-pencil test for science achievement can be made highly reliable, but still leave serious questions about its validity, as the basketball example suggested.

All assessment methods carry with them issues concerning practicality and cost. The cheapest and most practical test, especially for large-scale testing, is one that can be administered to a large group of students simultaneously in minimum time using the fewest materials. But again, the closer a test comes to this ideal, the more likely it is that its validity may come into question.

The most appropriate assessment method for any particular application may also vary with the purpose of the assessment. Generalizable, group-administered, context-invariant assessments, because they are relatively inexpensive, easy to administer, and easy to understand and interpret, are often considered more suitable for large-scale assessments for policy purposes. Individualized, longer, and more curriculum-embedded assessments are considered primarily for their value to the classroom teacher, because they are more complex and the results are usually used for diagnostic purposes. But because assessments for policy purposes need not involve every child, and may provide valid and reliable information on small population samples, there is little need for them to be simple, and the information lost by making them too generalizable may be greater than what is gained by the simplicity. My goal is not to elaborate further these arguments for or against the various types of methods on the basis of concerns such as reliability and validity, practicality and cost, or purpose of assessment. Instead, I lay out the methods that have been used effectively and illustrate them with examples from assessment contexts and other science education activities in which they have been used. My sympathy is with the use of a wide range of methods that come as close as possible to actual practice (Hein 1987, 1990).

A Survey of Assessment Methods

Observation

Observation is the oldest known scientific method for the study of nature. It was established long before science became a separate form of inquiry and is a common assessment tool for a wide variety of learning activities. In sports such as diving and gymnastics, in music competitions, and in crafts programs, observing what the learner does is a traditional as well as modern way of evaluating achievement. Complex types of learning, such as those just mentioned, and more mundane skills, such as using a measuring instrument or carrying out a filtration, are served equally well.

Psychologists from Itard to Piaget to the present have watched children and adults perform to determine their level of understanding or stage of development. Piaget (1929) argued that the only advantage his chosen method of clinical interviews had over observation was that it allowed the experimenter to contrive situations that might not occur as readily if children's behavior were simply observed. Otherwise, he said, observation would be an excellent research tool.

Duckworth's (1978) assessment of the African Primary Science Project is an example of the use of observation as the primary assessment tool. This curriculum project endeavored to introduce African elementary school children to science through materials-based, hands-on activities derived from a similar curriculum developed at the Elementary Science Study. Children observed the behavior of ant lions (an indigenous insect), worked with simple electricity, used classroom-constructed microscopes, and so on. What was the value of this program? Did the children who participated in the program learn anything that other children did not?

To answer these questions as an outside program evaluator, Duckworth set up a mock classroom that contained materials similar to, but different from, the ones used in the project. She divided the children into two groups, those who had participated in the project and those who had not. Then she observed each group's behavior in the mock classroom. What she saw was that students who had been part of the project interacted more with the science materials and used them in more complex ways than did the children who had followed the more textbook-oriented curriculum. She was even able to develop a rough quantitative scale of diversity/complexity to compare the work of the two groups. Her evaluation may have been helped by the fact that it was carried out in a culture that did not have an abundant supply of the kinds of materials that are common to hands-on science programs.

Several more recent science assessment schemes involve trained assessors observing what students do as they go about "doing" science. The Massachusetts State Department of Education devised performance tests for a stratified random sample of 3,000 4th and 8th grade students, which teachers administered in the spring of 1989. Students were asked to classify groups of objects, estimate the number of grains of popcorn in a container, and complete various measurement tasks. The teachers who acted as assessors were trained to observe the children's activities and write up what they observed.

These exercises were derived from the major British national assessment effort carried out by the Assessment of Performance Unit (APU), which I discuss in more detail below. Observing children doing science was an important component of the assessment, and the value of observations, as well as the difficulties associated with them, have been discussed at length in the annual and summary reports prepared as part of the APU work. For example, Harlen, Black, and Johnson (1981) describe an exercise in which 11-year-old children were given a mechanical caterpillar that crawled forward when wound up. After the children played with the toy for two or three minutes, they were asked whether they saw a connection between the number of times the wind-up key was turned and the distance traveled by the caterpillar. Trained testers watched the children and recorded each child's behavior on a prepared checklist. The APU group found observation difficult, but possible, given time to train the testers, forethought concerning the possible activities that children might undertake, and one-to-one test administration:

> In some cases it was not possible to decide whether, for instance, an action which apparently controlled a variable was deliberate or accidental, and in such cases the decision had to be left until later when the pupil's work was discussed with him. Using the check list was a skilled activity requiring intense concentration on the part of the tester, for a wavering of attention might result in an action being missed, with no opportunity to replay or recall the event. It was often a struggle to make sense of the pupil's action (what do you do when a pupil uses the string to tie the caterpillar's hat to the leg of a chair and proceeds to get the toy to tow the chair?) and it was the need for this close scrutiny that made one-to-one administration essential (Harlen, Black, and Johnson 1981, p. 115).

Verbal Responses

Verbal responses are a particularly useful way of finding out what students know, since they make up much of the day-to-day interchange between teachers and pupils. As more formal assessment methods, they also have their place. In the quotation above, for example, it is evident that testers talked with children and asked them why they carried out the actions they did. Researchers interested in children's concepts often conduct clinical interviews to investigate children's knowledge of and ideas about science. In advanced degree work in all fields, oral examinations in which candidates and professors engage in discussion to find out what the student knows are standard practice.

Churchill and Petner (1977) suggested that children's spontaneous conversations can be a guide to their science knowledge. And Chittenden (1990) has studied the idea of group conversations as a basis of classroom assessment. He suggests that teachers carry on conversations with an entire classroom of students, following a few guidelines:

- that discussion begin with open-ended questions, such as:
  - What have you noticed lately about our caterpillars?
  - What are some things you know about shadows? What is a shadow?
  - What sorts of questions do you have about the sun? What have you wondered about?
- that teachers refrain from correcting or unduly modifying the children's comments

  • that discussions proceed in a manner ensuring the involvement of
most all of the children
    • that records be made of each child's statements (Chittenden 1990,
p. 221).

The guidelines are intended to encourage the sort of discussion that is
sustained by child-initiated questions and ideas, and that allows children
some control over the direction of the conversation.

Chittenden characterizes the discussions as "staged observations"
that attempt to capture a dimension of classroom life that ordinarily
remains undocumented—namely children's talk. Dyasi (1990) has also
analyzed transcripts of teacher-student conversations to gain an
understanding of children's approaches to science. He sees the recorded
discussions as an important component of the documentation of students'
learning, part of a portfolio describing students' progress.

Formal recording of conversations requires considerable resources.
If observation requires one-to-one interaction, then guiding and
recording conversations requires more than a one-to-one ratio of
assessors to groups of students. Although conversations can be recorded
on tape, they still need to be listened to, possibly transcribed, and
analyzed. Nevertheless, children's verbal responses can be made part of
classroom assessment. Even if carried out less formally than would be
required for research purposes, they can provide the teacher with
information on what children know and understand, and notes from such
conversations can be part of an assessment system. Several curriculum
development projects suggest that teachers talk with students both
before a science unit is introduced and after it is completed. The first
conversation helps teachers assess students' baseline knowledge, and the
second conversation gives them the opportunity to determine how
students' knowledge has changed.

Written Records

Written responses from students are a simple and direct way to
assess learning; in fact, they are the most common form of academic
assessment. Our reliance on multiple-choice and other short-answer
tests, however, may make us forget that written tests can take many
forms, from completing sentences, arranging statements, and making lists
to providing explanations for answers, composing essays, and drafting
reports. Carlson (1987) provides examples of ten common types of
written examinations, including many specific examples from secondary
science education.

The General Certificate of Secondary Education (GCSE), which was introduced in all British state-supported secondary schools in 1988, uses a variety of short and long written response methods, as well as practical tests, to assess learning (Department of Education and Science 1985).

Written work can reflect students' science knowledge without being specifically part of an assessment task. Thus, Rockcastle (1986) argued that essays may provide considerable insight into students' science knowledge. He uses as an example stories children wrote in response to the prompt to describe what their school might look like more than 100 years from now, considering the effects of biological succession. More test-like are the explanations children give for their answers to test questions. A common type of question used on APU tests and GCSE examinations asks students not only to give an answer, but also to provide one or more reasons for their answer. An entire category of the APU scheme concerns planning investigations. Students are presented with a problem, provided with a written list or pictures of material they might use to solve the problem, and asked how they would go about doing so (see Figure 7.1).

FIGURE 7.1

Suppose you are going to make a chopping board to use for cutting bread or chopping vegetables or meat. You have to decide which is the best kind of wood to use. You have blocks of four different kinds of wood (A, B, C, D) and you can use any of the things in the picture below to do some tests on them. (You don't have to use all the things).

What would you do to:

> Test the blocks to find out which kind of wood is best for making a chopping board.

Make sure you say   (1) which things you would use (2) what you would do (3) how you would find out the result

_____

_____

_____

A number of APU practical tasks requiring written responses were adapted by the National Assessment of Educational Progress (NAEP) and tried out in the United States (Blomberg et al. 1986). NAEP (1987) published a popular version of these methods for teachers.

Written responses can also be the result of actual science work. Students can be asked to carry out various tasks that will result in answers to given questions; if students perform the tasks correctly, they should come up with the correct written answers. In several assessments of measurement skills, including the ones carried out in New York State and Massachusetts and by the APU, students are given a thermometer or other scale to read, or a ruler and an item to measure, and then asked questions such as "How long is this item?" or "What is the reading on this scale?" The written test paper can be used as evidence of the student's degree of success at the task.

Drawing

Through illustration, students can demonstrate an idea or concept or show that they have learned a skill. They may sketch what a product looks like, describe an apparatus by detailed drawings or diagrams, depict a situation, or illustrate their beliefs. As an assessment tool, drawing can range from the most artistic, free expression to the precise rendering of technical details. Dyasi (1990) has analyzed drawings that are part of the portfolios of students' work from the Prospect Archive and discussed how they can be used to provide information about students' knowledge of science. In my own work (Hein 1985), I found that teachers could test students' knowledge of how to use a microscope simply by asking them to draw what they saw through the microscope (see Figure 7.2).

Products

Practical work in science often leads to products. And examining the products of students' practical work can indicate what students have learned. If an animal is cared for, if a doll house is wired and the lights work (a final assessment task for a curriculum unit on electricity), if the product of the chemical reaction is crystalline and pure, we can make inferences about a student's level of performance and understanding.

The APU surveys used products in an ingenious way. Students at each of the three age levels were asked to carry out multistep procedures that resulted in a product. The purpose of one such activity, building a simple kaleidoscope from folded paper, tape, and mirrors, was not to

FIGURE 7.2
Student Drawings

Part Two
Draw a picture in the circle below of what sand looks like through a microscope.

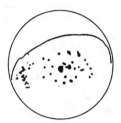

Part Two
Draw a picture in the circle below of what sand looks like through a microscope.

Part Three
Draw a picture in the circle below of what you would see in a drop of water taken from a pond, when you looked at it under a microscope.

Part Three
Draw a picture in the circle below of what you would see in a drop of water taken from a pond, when you looked at it under a microscope.

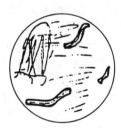

Pretest
MOS Kits Evalution1986

Post-test
MOS Kits Evalution1986

produce the product, but to determine how well students could follow instructions. In other assessment schemes, such as those developed in Connecticut (Baron 1989), students are asked, individually or in groups, to carry out both short-term (less than one period) and long-term tasks (over several days to several weeks) that result in a product so that teachers can evaluate students' knowledge.

In summary, we can assess students in a variety of ways: we can observe what they do, listen to what they say, read what write, and analyze what they produce. Any behavior that can be perceived can be adapted for assessment. The typical written, short-answer test is just one point on the continuum of assessment.

An Assessment System: The APU

Much of the literature critical of present science assessment practices argues not only for *alternatives* to multiple-choice tests, but also for a *variety* of methods to assess student performance. The most extensive model for such an alternative assessment for large-scale national policy purposes is provided by the APU (Black 1987), which systematically collected data on British student achievement for over a decade. Established by the Department of Education and Science in 1975 "to promote the development of methods of assessing and monitoring the achievement of children in schools and to seek to identify the incidence of underachievement" (quoted in Harlen et al. 1981), the APU conducted national achievement surveys in certain school subjects. The APU science monitoring teams began their work in 1977 and developed an assessment framework based on the proposition that "science is to be regarded as a mode of thought and activity which may be encountered in a number of subjects appearing in the school subject."

In five annual surveys of schools from 1980 to 1984, the APU collected 3,750,000 responses from 240,000 pupils aged 11, 13, and 15 in 7,500 schools across England, Wales, and Northern Ireland (a 2 percent sample). The surveys provide a fairly detailed description of the level of science competence of British students, and the methodologies and outcomes of the surveys have profoundly influenced the new National Curriculum, which was introduced into all Welsh and English state schools in fall 1989. The APU work has provided insight into students' understanding of concepts, pioneered evaluation methodologies, and spawned major research programs based on both the findings and the methodology of the surveys.

In designing the overall plan to survey science achievement, the APU tried to take into account that science is primarily a way of doing things, and only partially a collection of facts and concepts. The group set up a six-part scheme to describe science and then developed different kinds of assessment strategies for each component (see Figure 7.3).

FIGURE 7.3
The Categories of Science Performance

1. Use of graphical and symbolic representation	— reading information from graphs, tables, and charts	written test
	— representing information as graphs, tables, and charts	
2. Use of apparatus and measuring instruments	— using measuring instruments	group practical test
	— estimating physical quantities	
	— following instructions for practical work	
3. Observation	— making and interpreting observations	group practical test
4. Interpretation and application	— i interpreting presented information	written test
	— ii applying: Biology concepts Physics concepts Chemistry concepts	
5. Planning of investigations	— planning parts of investigations	written test
	— planning entire investigations	
6. Performance of investigations	— performing entire investigations	individual practical test

---

In the APU scheme, assessment of science knowledge and concepts is limited to categories 4 (Interpretation and application) and 5 (Planning of investigations); the other categories focus on processes. The actual interdependence of concepts and processes (as well as a third component, attitude or interest) was recognized by the group at the beginning of the assessment and repeatedly reinforced by the results. Nevertheless, to the extent that the categories can be separated, the APU approach does so.

The practical tests for category 2 were usually administered to groups of students at stations set up in a classroom. Students went from station to station and carried out the measurements and other tasks as directed. Category 6 tasks were administered one to one. The wooden board example in Figure 7.1 was used as both a practical test and a planning exercise, as were dozens of other tasks. Students were given materials and equipment and asked to demonstrate which piece of wood made the best cutting board. The written sections varied with the different categories and included many alternatives to short-answer questions. Figures 7.4 and 7.5 illustrate other types of questions that were used in this assessment.

Assessment Methods in Research and Curriculum Development

If we wish to probe children's science beliefs, or understand how concepts develop, we have to find out what children know. Similarly, in order to assess the value of any science curriculum, we have to find out what students learn from using the curriculum. One way to gauge the adequacy of the current state of science assessment is to examine the extent to which curriculum developers and researchers interested in children's understanding of science employ current tests in their work. The curriculum groups provide a particularly appropriate touchstone, since their goal is to introduce new materials into existing schools. We can also look at what assessment tools the curriculum developers actually employ as they produce science materials and introduce these materials into the classroom.

In general, newer science curriculum materials advocate assessments that:
  • are embedded within instructional materials,
  • use a variety of methods to assess the student's progress,
  • emphasize teacher observation and teacher judgment,
  • provide methods for getting at the reasons behind children's answers.

For example, The Improving Urban Elementary Science (IUES) project (Harmon and Mokros 1990) uses a general assessment framework for all its units. At the start of instruction, the teacher gives students a

FIGURE 7.4
APU Sample Questions

Category 5: Planning of Investigations (Age 13)

A group of pupils are comparing water from two different towns. They want to do a test to find out which kind of water lathers more easily with soap flakes.

If they want to make it a *fair* test they will have to make sure that some things in the test are the same for both kinds of water. Suggest *three* things that should be the same:

1. _____

_____

2. _____

_____

3. _____

_____

Category 4: Interpretation and Application (Age 11)

Walking along this footpath, Thomas noticed that there was ivy growing on the trees, but only around three-quarters of the trunks. None of the trees had ivy growing on the side nearest to the path.

Think of *two* different reasons why the ivy might grown only on some sides of the trees. Write the first under (a) and the second under (b).

(a) I think it might be because_____

_____

(b) I think it might be because _____

_____

pre-unit questionnaire to gather baseline information about their knowledge of the subject. The questionnaire requires writing and drawing as well as short answers. While carrying out the unit, the teacher is advised to observe certain aspects of students' behavior as evidence of learning, and assessment modes are provided through the course of the unit, including embedded assessments. "An embedded assessment is not a test. It is one of the daily learning experiences written in a special format" (EDC 1989). At the end of the unit, both written and performance assessments are provided. In a 6th grade unit on structures, in which children build towers and other architectural objects and examine what makes structures stand, an embedded assessment involves building bridges; the final performance assessment requires students to design and build a model of a playground (EDC 1989). The written items in the assessment sections ask students to draw features of structures and to explain what they understand concepts to mean; they also provide many opportunities for open-ended responses.

Thus, the project materials include two kinds of assessment activities. One category involves tasks that are part of the curriculum and that provide feedback to teachers (and to others) as students progress. Another category constitutes more formal assessment at the end of a set of activities to provide summary information on what students have learned. The written material for the assessment component of the unit emphasizes that a multiplicity of methods is not only desirable but necessary to find out what children have learned during the course of the varied hands-on activities contained in the unit.

A similar multiplicity of assessment methods characterizes the work of other research groups interested in understanding children's science concepts. Some typical methods include the following:

Clinical Interviews: This method, so brilliantly employed by Piaget, is still extensively used. Carey's (1985) insights into children's understanding of living things, obtained primarily through interviews, is a fine example. In some instances children are interviewed without being shown any prompts; in other cases they respond to drawings, photographs, or objects, or to questions about an activity they have carried out.

Drawing: Students' understanding of the nature of light has been explored by a number of research groups using, among other methods, the simple device of asking students to draw what happens when the eye sees an object (Anderson 1983, Chittenden 1984, Osborne et al. 1990).

FIGURE 7.5
APU Sample Questions

Category 4: Applying Chemistry Concepts (Age 13)

A smooth marble fountain was built in the middle of a city.

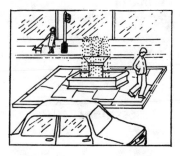

After several years, the surface of the marble was worn and covered with small holes.

Think of three reasons, other than damage by people, which could have caused the small holes to form.

1. _____

2. _____

3. _____

Category 4: Applying Chemistry Concepts (Age 15)

A piece of phosphorous was held in a flask as shown in the diagram. The mass of the flask and contents equalled 205 g. The sun's rays were focused on the phosphorous, which then caught fire. The white smoke produced slowly dissolved in the water.

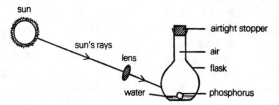

After cooking, the flask and its contents were weighed again.

1. Would you expect the weight to be
   ___ A. more than 205 g.   ___ B. 205 g.
   ___ C. less than 205 g.   ___ D. not enough information to answer

2. Give the reason for your answer:

   _____

   _____

Performance. In a series of experiments intended to discover young adults' and adults' understanding of physical forces, McClusky (1983) asked individuals to walk across a room and drop an object at the appropriate moment so that it would land in a container. Driver (1990) has summarized the status of research on conceptual development and its relationship to science assessment.

Researchers interested in exploring students' understanding of science usually use assessments that go far beyond the boundaries of traditional tests and they rarely use multiple-choice questions.

Assessment Issues

Comparing Methods

An obvious issue raised by the availability of such a wide range of assessment methods is whether different methods provide similar or different results. Are data resulting from different types of questions comparable? Do performance measures provide the same information as written measures, only in a different form? Much evidence suggests that even small changes in the framing of questions leads to significantly different results. In the first International Educational Assessment, students answered both multiple-choice questions and practical questions in science. The authors concluded:

> Perhaps of special interest, in view of the current debate on the place to be accorded to practical work of various kinds in school science, was the attempt to produce optional tests of practical abilities requiring only very simple and easily obtainable materials. Unfortunately, only two countries elected to take these "practical" tests, but the evidence from these suggests that such practical tests measure quite different abilities from those assessed by more traditional tests, even those designed to assess practical skills as far as possible without resort to actual apparatus (Comber and Keeves 1973).

In 1984-85 a statewide assessment in Connecticut included both performance testing and multiple-choice items. In one item, reproduced in Figure 7.6, the percentage of correct responses was reduced from 71 percent to only 5 percent when 4th grade students were asked to demonstrate how they would hold the coins rather than choose the correct answer from the list of responses (Baron 1986).

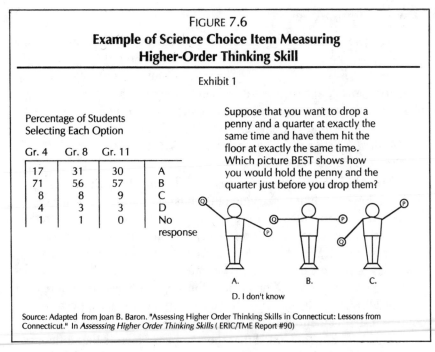

FIGURE 7.6
**Example of Science Choice Item Measuring
Higher-Order Thinking Skill**

Exhibit 1

Percentage of Students
Selecting Each Option

Gr. 4	Gr. 8	Gr. 11	
17	31	30	A
71	56	57	B
8	8	9	C
4	3	3	D
1	1	0	No response

Suppose that you want to drop a penny and a quarter at exactly the same time and have them hit the floor at exactly the same time. Which picture BEST shows how you would hold the penny and the quarter just before you drop them?

A.   B.   C.

D. I don't know

Source: Adapted from Joan B. Baron. "Assessing Higher Order Thinking Skills in Connecticut: Lessons from Connecticut." In *Assesssing Higher Order Thinking Skills* (ERIC/TME Report #90)

Badger and Thomas (1989) report significant differences in responses to multiple-choice items and open-ended written questions in their analysis of results from Massachusetts. The APU reports that for similar questions, response rates are, from lowest to highest, as follows:

- written response to questions presented in words
- written response with an illustration
- written response with actual equipment to look at
- written response after actual practical work
- observing the students working.

The Model of Science

Using varied types of assessments more adequately reflects the multifaceted nature of science, and it sets a more appropriate example for the kind of science that should be taught in schools. If a state, a school district, or a national agency advocates hands-on science in the curriculum (as most do), assessment methods should reflect the science described in curriculum guidelines. For example, if a major goal of science teaching is to increase skills for solving poorly defined problems, then students should be required to practice these skills and be assessed for their competence in this area

What Is Being Assessed

The use of assessment techniques that actively involve students in doing science gives us the added benefit of beginning to understand the complex factors that influence performance. Multiple-choice questions, no matter how carefully constructed and how extensively field-tested, must of necessity hide a wide range of reasons for different responses. The thinking behind students' answers can only be inferred from the limited data. For this reason, research groups generally avoid multiple-choice questions.

The APU has field-tested thousands of items through a combination of techniques, trying out similar questions in a range of formats. It has concluded that even very subtle differences in illustration, presentation, or content may profoundly change the way in which students respond. Whether questions are set in a "scientific" or "everyday" context can change answer rates and greatly influence gender differences in responses. When a question stem includes material related to a social issue, students' ability to generalize is diminished because the content distracts them from the data (Donnelly and Welford 1989).

The APU has concluded that the number of factors that influence response rates is so great that we cannot predict, even among questions of similar types, which ones will be easier or harder for particular groups of students. In reviewing the research on science concepts, McDermott (1984) found that certain factors, shown in Figure 7.7, have to be considered when carrying out research on conceptual understanding. These same issues are relevant to science assessment.

Relationship to Instruction. The close relationship between assessment strategies and instruction is supported by using a variety of assessment methods. Since good science instruction invariably involves students' active participation in constructing knowledge in collaboration with their teacher, the passive quality of multiple-choice tests disrupts the instructional flow. It is a separate activity, bringing with it the typical qualities of "testing": anxiety, comparison between pupils, and a change in mood and classroom climate. As the curriculum projects discussed above illustrate, the use of a wider range of assessment methods allows testing to be embedded into the curriculum.

A wider range of assessment strategies also allows teachers to better understand each student's level of comprehension or skill attainment. Teachers know that the extra time needed to grade problems, read essays, or assess constructions (in comparison to marking multiple-choice

FIGURE 7.7
Characteristics of Research on Conceptual Understanding

Because results and methods are so closely intertwined in research on conceptual understanding, it is important in interpreting the findings to bear in mind the procedures used. Characteristics that should be considered in interpreting the results of a particular project include:

Nature of instrument used to assess understanding. How actively involved was the student in the task? The responses a student makes in writing answers to printed questions may not be the same as those triggered when the student is observing a demonstration, using a computer, or manipulating apparatus in the laboratory.

Degree of interaction between student and investigator. Was it possible for the investigator to clarify student responses? Through further questioning during an interview, an investigator may verify the meaning of a particular response and follow up on comments indicating unsuspected difficulties. On the other hand, during a written examination a student's responses are unlikely to be influenced by what the investigator does or says.

Depth of probing. In how much detail did the investigator examine student understanding? The investigator's perception of student thinking may differ if only one question is asked about a concept rather than many, or if only one context is used rather than several. Results based solely on a student' initial responses may be different from those obtained when the student has the opportunity to consider alternatives.

Form of data. What kinds of data were obtained—for example, written responses to questions, transcripts of interviews, classroom observations? Administering written questions to large numbers of students is useful in determining the frequency of misconceptions in different populations. In contract, the highly interactive structure of an individual interview allows the investigator to examine in detail the nature of a particular difficulty.

Physical setting. In what ways did the environment in which a study was conducted affect the results? A specially designed experimental setting allows an investigator to focus on a given student's understanding a particular concept. However, observing the interaction among students in the more natural setting of the classroom may provide a broader perspective on the range of student beliefs.

Time frame. At what point in instruction was a particular test administered? Over what period of time was the whole study conducted? The significance of particular results may depend on whether tests were administered before, during, or after instruction. Results based on a single administration of a test may differ from those obtained with more extensive testing.

Goals of investigator. How did the perspective of the investigator affect the design of the study or the way in which the data were interpreted? For those who teach physics, the primary motivation in undertaking this kind of research is often the improvement of instruction. For others, the emphasis may be on developing models of human thought. Similar data may be used by some investigators to identify and describe specific difficulties and by others to infer the conceptual framework within which an individual views the physical world.

questions) is compensated for by the insights gained; teachers find out how students tackle problems. A wider range of methods is also necessary if an assessment system is to be applicable to students of all abilities and from all ethnic and social backgrounds. Repeated studies have demonstrated (Meier 1973, Haney 1978) that all kinds of examination and assessment questions can be misunderstood. Only in formats where the assessor can understand the reasons for the answers students have given can cultural and linguistic misunderstandings be analyzed and valid assessments made of the knowledge of all students (Harmon and Mokros 1990).

Assessment Portfolios. Recognition of the need for a variety of assessment methods has led to proposals that assessment be based on a collection of a student's work, a portfolio of materials, rather than by the "blurred snapshot" provided by a single test (Collins 1990). Portfolios of student work have been a cornerstone of the assessment of student progress at the Prospect School, in North Bennington, Vermont, for 20 years, and have been recommended by such diverse agencies as the Coalition of Essential Schools (Wiggins 1989), the Task Group on Assessment and Testing (Black 1987) as part of the English National Curriculum, the Connecticut State Department of Education (Baron et al. 1989), and a task force considering assessment for the Boston Public Schools (*Boston Globe* 1989). Portfolios or profiles may constitute one component of the British CGSE assessment (Brown 1988) and represent a major part of one approved scheme, in which the students assess much of their work themselves (Davis 1989).

Formative and Summative Assessment. A useful distinction can be made between ongoing assessment, during the course of a semester to assist a teacher in preparing lessons and helping students to learn, and final assessments, usually at the end of a unit or year to find out what has been accomplished. The former are formative and the latter summative assessments. Externally developed and administered tests are often considered more appropriate for summative assessments because they avoid the danger of teacher bias and may provide comparable information for a range of classrooms. However, *cumulative* formative assessments that provide evidence over a longer period of time can be just as objective and comparable across classrooms or districts. These might included samples of students' work from an entire semester, evidence for achievement based on carefully defined criteria, or the portfolios mentioned above.

Relationship to Inservice Training. There is obvious value for inservice education in the kinds of data that result from more extensive children's responses to science probes. Churchill and Petner (1977), Chittenden (1990), and many others have explicitly made use of such information for inservice work. Much of the APU assessment was carried out by classroom teachers, and the major portion of the assessment that will form one component of the new national curriculum will also be in the hands of classroom teachers.

The Task Group on Assessment and Testing, in its recommendations for carrying out assessment at the national level (Black 1987), has proposed a process of *moderation*, a process by which groups of teachers at various levels—the grade, the school, or the district—get together and discuss results and compare grading standards, especially on the more complex open-ended questions and performance measures. The proposed moderation scheme assures that grading will converge on a uniform set of standards, and it serves as a continuing inservice activity for teachers. Practicing professionals would do more than compare student achievement from school to school; they would also compare their own understandings and standards with those of colleagues.

Conclusions

As we have seen, there are diverse methods available for assessing science learning and a wide range of contexts in which these assessments have been used. Many ways of empirically assessing student learning have been developed and applied directly either to classroom-based or larger-scale assessments. The problem of introducing these methods into schools and school systems on a national scale, however, has clearly not been solved.

Changing school practices in any area is a difficult process. Factors ranging from the ordinary inertia inherent in any system to the particular political forces that come to bear on education make it difficult to bring about change. One necessary condition for change is the demonstrated existence of viable alternative practices. They do exist in the field of science assessment. Other components that are needed for such a change include the following:

1. *Time.* Schools and school systems need to embark on systematic, long-term programs to change the nature of assessment. Some of the strategies proposed by state departments and some school reform groups point in this direction. Current testing based on multiple-choice, short-answer questions is established, teachers teach with it in mind, students expect it, and parents and administrators are used to the form of

the results. In order to make a change, every constituency needs time to get acclimatized to the new models.

2. *Time-out.* Time is not enough; "time-out"—a chance to try out new assessment methods without the pressure of performance and accountability based on the old system—is also important. It is unrealistic to expect any responsible educator to embrace a wholly new form of assessment, with uncertain results, as long as funding, professional advancement and perhaps even job review are based on the outcomes of an older system that is to be replaced. Schools and school systems need trial time, a chance to modify practices without the expectation of immediate success and positive results.

The kinds of assessment discussed in this chapter represent a major change in school practice, so they will cause some disruption before they are established. In Great Britain, the new national assessments that accompany the national curriculum will be phased in gradually, with the first year of national testing (at one age level) in 1991 carried out as unreported results, so the first assessment will not take place until 1992, three years after the first children have entered under the new guidelines.

3. *Education.* If we want to change the assessment methods used in schools, then the entire population involved needs to be educated to accept and implement the changes. A new kind of assessment requires rethinking and refocusing. If teachers are to collect portfolios of work, if principals are to receive and to prepare narrative reports of student progress, if state agencies are to make decisions based on a different kind of evidence, it is not enough to argue that this new system is better, provides more valid information, or will be more useful in the long run. We must also provide workshops, inservice training, and time for all the constituencies to discuss and understand the methods and their implications. Most educators believe they know how to interpret the results from multiple-choice science tests, if for no other reason than they have become so familiar with them, that they can relate the results of the tests with their experience. A similar body of knowledge and common understanding needs to be developed for alternative assessments with the different quality of information these will provide.

4. *Resources.* Change requires resources: teacher education, administrator education, public awareness, and a recognition that assessment is a form of passing judgment and can never be made totally objective. It requires a component of professional judgment to interpret the results.

Responsible assessment is a difficult and delicate process. It constantly faces competition from simplistic methods that appear to be more efficient, but are inadequate for carrying out the same task. To establish and preserve valid assessment practices, educators, politicians, and the public need to make a concerted effort to champion a range of methods. The methods are available, and they provide the kind of information that makes for useful debate and discussion. But debate and discussion are not enough. If we intend to improve the way science is taught—as our national education goals claim we do—we must also improve the way it is assessed: active science demands active assessment.

References

Anderson, C.W., and E.L. Smith. (1986). *Children's Conceptions of Light and Color: Understanding the Role of Unseen Rays*. East Lansing, Mich.: Institute for Research on Teaching, Research Series #166.

Assessment of Performance Unit, Science Project. (1989). *Selected Bibliography of APU Publications, 1985–1989*. London: APU Science, Centre for Educational Studies, Kings College.

Badger, E., and B. Thomas. (1989). *On Their Own: Student Response to Open-Ended Tests in Science*. Quincy, Mass.: Massachusetts Department of Education.

Black, P. (1987). *Report: National Curriculum: Task Group on Assessment and Testing*. London: Department of Education and Science.

Black, P. (1990). "Looking to the Future." Lecture presented at the Association for Science Education meeting, Lancaster, England, January 6.

Baron, J.B. (1986). "Assessing High Order Thinking Skills in Connecticut." In *Assessing High Order Thinking Skills*. Princeton, N.J.: Educational Testing Service.

Baron, J.B., P.D. Forgione, Jr., D.A. Rindone, H. Kruglanski, and B. Davey. (1989). "Towards a New Generation of Student Outcome Measures: Connecticut's Common Core of Learning Assessment." Paper presented at AERA Annual Meeting, San Francisco, Calif.

Blomberg, F., M. Epstein, W. McDonald, and I. Mullis. (1986). *A Pilot Study of Higher Order Thinking Skills Assessment Techniques in Science and Mathematics: Final Report, Parts 1 and 2*. Princeton, N.J.: National Assessment of Educational Progress.

Boston Globe. (Dec. 12, 1989). "New Academic Tests for Hub Pupils Proposed."

Brown, P. (1988). "Pupil Profiles." In *Assessment At 16*, edited by K. Selkirk. London: Routledge.

Carey, S. (1985). *Conceptual Change in Childhood*. Cambridge, Mass.: MIT Press.

Carlson, S.B. (1987). *Creative Classroom Testing*. Princeton, N.J.: Educational Testing Service.

Champagne, A.B., B.E. Lovitts, and B.J. Calinger. (1990). *Assessment in the Service of Instruction*. Washington, D.C.: American Association for the Advancement of Science.

Chittenden, E., et al. (1984). "A Pilot Study of Science Assessment." Unpublished manuscript. Princeton, N.J.: Educational Testing Service.

Chittenden, E. (1990). "Young Children's Discussions of Science Topics." In *The Assessment of Hands-on Elementary Science Programs*, edited by G.E. Hein. Grand Forks, N.D.: North Dakota Study Group on Evaluation.

Churchill, E.H.E., and J.H. Petner, Jr. (1977). *Children's Language and Thinking: A Report of Work-in-Progress*. Grand Forks, N.D.: North Dakota Study Group on Evaluation.

Collins, A. (1990). "Portfolios for Assessing Student Learning in Science: A New Name for a Familiar Idea." In *Assessment in the Service of Instruction*, edited by A.B. Champagne, B.E. Lovitts, and B.J. Calinger. Washington, D.C.: American Association for the Advancement of Science.

Comber, L.C., and J.P. Keeves. (1973). *Science Education in Nineteen Countries*. New York: Wiley.

Davis, A., and J. Armstrong. (1990). "State Initiatives in Science Assessment." In *Assessment in the Service of Instruction*, edited by A.B. Champagne, B.E. Lovitts, and B.J. Calinger. Washington, D.C.: American Association for the Advancement of Science.

Department of Education and Science. (1985). *General Certificate of Secondary Education, The National Criteria*. London: Her Majesty's Printing Office.

Donnelly, J.F., and A.G. Welford. (1989). "Assessing Pupils' Ability to Generalize." *International Journal of Science Education* 11: 161–171.

Driver, R. (1990). "Assessing the Progress of Children's Understanding in Science: A Developmental Perspective." In *The Assessment of Hands-on Elementary Science Programs*, edited by G.E. Hein. Grand Forks, N.D.: North Dakota Study Group on Evaluation.

Duckworth, E. (1978). *The African Primary Science Program: An Evaluation*. Grand Forks, N.D.: North Dakota Study Group on Evaluation.

Dyasi, H.M. (1990). "Children's Investigations of Natural Phenomena: A Source of Data for Assessment in Elementary School Science." In *The Assessment of Hands-on Elementary Science Programs*, edited by G.E. Hein. Grand Forks, N.D.: North Dakota Study Group on Evaluation.

Education Development Center. (1989). *Structures, Field Test Version*. Newton, Mass.: EDC.

Haney, W., and L. Scott. (1978). *Talking with Children about Testing: A Pilot Study of Test Item Ambiguity*. Cambridge, Mass.: National Consortium on Testing, Staff Circular #7, Huron Institute.

Harlen, W., P. Black, and S. Johnson. (1981). *Science in Schools, Age 11: Report No. 1*. London: Department of Education and Science.

Harmon, M., and J. Mokros. (1990). "Assessment of the New NSF Elementary Science Curricula, An Emerging Role." In *The Assessment of Hands-on Elementary Science Programs*, edited by G.E. Hein. Grand Forks, N.D.: North Dakota Study Group on Evaluation.

Harmon, M., J. Mokros, G. Dawson, M. Hartwig, R. Henderson, L. Lowery, and Z. Taylor. (1988). "Comments on the Need for New Assessment Materials." Informal document. Washington, D.C.: National Science Foundation.

Hein, G.E. (1985). *Final Evaluation of the Museum of Science KITS Program*. Cambridge, Mass.: Program Evaluation and Research Group, Lesley College.

Hein, G.E. (October 25, 1987). "The Right Test for Hands-On Learning." *Science and Children*, pp. 8–12.

Hein, G.E., ed. (1990). *The Assessment of Hands-On Elementary Science Programs*. Grand Forks, N.D.: North Dakota Study Group on Evaluation.

Jones, L.V. (1989). "School Achievement Trends in Mathematics and Science, and What Can Be Done to Improve Them." In *Review of Research in Education*, edited by E.Z. Rothkopf. Washington, D.C.: American Educational Research Association.

Knapp, M.S., et al. (1987). *Opportunities for Strategic Investment in K–12 Science Education*. Menlo Park, Calif.: SRI International.

McClusky, M. (1983). "Intuitive Physics." *Scientific American* 248: 122–130.

McDermott, L.C. (July 1984). "Research on Conceptual Understanding in Physics." *Physics Today* 24-32.

Meier, D. (1973). *Reading Failure and the Tests*. New York, N.Y.: Workshop Center for Open Education.

Murnane, R.J., and S.A. Raizen, eds. (1988). *Improving Indicators for the Quality of Science and Mathematics Education in Grades K–12*. Washington, D.C.: National Academy Press.

National Assessment of Educational Progress. (1987). *Learning by Doing*. Report No. 17-HOS-80. Princeton, N.J.: Educational Testing Service.

Osborne, J., P. Black, M. Smith, and J. Medows. (1990). *Light*. Liverpool: SPACE Project, Liverpool U. Press.

Piaget, J. (1929). *The Child's Conception of the World*. London: Routledge & Kegan Paul.

Raizen, S., J.B. Baron, A.B. Champagne, E. Haertel, I.N.V. Mullis, and J. Oakes. (1989). *Assessment in Elementary School Science Education*. Washington, D.C.: National Center for Improving Science Education.

Resnick, L. (1987). *Education and Learning to Think*. Washington, D.C.: National Academy Press.

Rockcastle, V.N. (1986). "Nothing Succeeds Like Succession." *Science and Children* 24: 20–24.

Stenzel, N. (1988). "Assessment of Science Process Skills at the State Level." Paper presented at AERA annual meeting, New Orleans, La.

Wiggins, G. (1989). "A True Test: Towards More Authentic and Equitable Assessment." *Phi Delta Kappan* 70: 703–713.

8

The Intellectual Costs of Secrecy in Mathematics Assessment

Judah L. Schwartz

What price do we pay to ensure that mathematics assessments remain unavailable for public scrutiny? The price is high, and we pay it several times over in our different capacities: as members of a society that is profoundly undereducated and incapacitated in dealing with public policy matters that have quantitative dimensions; as learners in a school system that does not have sufficient freedom to challenge us to think inventively and creatively about mathematics; and as teachers and parents who are torn between educating our youngsters richly and imaginatively and preparing them to demonstrate their competence on tests that are deeply flawed.

I do not claim that all the ills of current methods of accountability assessment in mathematics are due to the nonpublic nature of the instruments. I do claim that many of the ills that do not result directly from the secrecy of the instruments are nonetheless indirect consequences of the secrecy and are substantially exacerbated by it.

Because the field of assessment has heard more than its share of bleating about the ills and evils of educational testing, I sketch here what I believe to be a viable and pragmatic approach to assessment that is not flawed in the ways our current methods of assessing mathematics teaching and learning are.

This chapter is adapted from Judah L. Schwartz and Katherine Viator, ed., "The Prices of Secrecy: The Social, Intellectual, and Psychological Costs of Current Assessment Practice," a Report to the Ford Foundation (Cambridge: Educational Technology Center, Harvard Graduate School of Education, September 1990).

Holding the System Accountable: How We Do It Now

Most state departments of education and local school boards depend heavily on the results of standardized multiple-choice tests to make judgments and reach conclusions about how well various school systems and individual schools are educating youngsters mathematically. Even the U.S. Department of Education makes extensive use of the results of these tests. And much of the uproar about our youngsters' mathematical incapacity is due to media reports about poor performance on just such tests.

What I find remarkable is that these reports never contain examples of the test questions. *The media do not publish the questions: They publish reports about students' performance on the questions.* But I must not be too hasty in criticizing the media. For the most part, the tests are not available to them to publish. Like the general public, the media cannot purchase, or even see, copies of the tests that are used to report on the health of the schools. Thus, people read and hear about student performance, but they don't have access to the test questions, the scoring criteria and procedures, or the methods of aggregating performances on subtests into a single or small group of numbers.

Can we be well served by such procedures? We might be, if we were willing to trust the testing companies to produce tests that are free of erroneous and unambiguous questions and to grade them in error-free ways. In the spirit of the ancient adage "this above all—do no damage," can the test makers be trusted to introduce no faulty questions or answers?

Commercial manufacturers of standardized tests are generally well-respected organizations with long traditions of involvement in education; many, in fact, are also textbook publishers. They employ experts on the various academic subjects, consult other professionals about putting together the tests, and rely on still other specialists to review the tests before they are used. It would seem reasonable to assume, then, that they can be trusted to design error-free tests.

While not wishing to cast aspersions on the integrity or good intentions of the test manufacturers, I must point out that in almost every field of intellectual endeavor there is publicly available literature in which findings are reported, discussed, and debated. Results that are flawed are, by virtue of open discussion, ultimately exposed and discarded. No journal in the natural sciences, for instance, would accept for publication an article that contained the results of measurements made with instruments whose internal structures could not be publicly examined, debated, and evaluated.

Assessment in education is quite different: tests are prepared and administered without the scrutiny of the community that ultimately depends on the results that the tests report. Occasionally, detected errors appear in front-page stories in the *New York Times* about some ingenious high school student who slew the Princeton dragon. But do we know how many errors go undetected?

Here is a charming example from a test for high school students that was designed by one of the most prominent American testing organizations:

> Two identical coins are placed flat on a table and in contact with one another. One of the coins is held still while the other is rolled without slipping all the way around the circumference of the stationary coin until it returns to its original position. How many turns does the rolling coin make?

Students were offered a choice of five answers; none was correct, even though the question and all the answers had been extensively reviewed by the organization's internal experts and external consultants. Apparently, nobody had actually tried rolling the coin to verify the answer (which I suggest you do if you think you've calculated the answer).

Even if the problem of error in questions and answers were resolved, the costs of using nonpublic assessments would still be high, for other issues are involved.

A continuing concern of every teacher and curriculum designer is the level and tone of the instructional materials they write and present to students. This is as it should be. These materials are influenced by many sources, including the tests that are used to judge how well the instructional system is meeting its objectives. This, too, is as it should be. If the level and tone of the instructional materials prepared for our youngsters are influenced by the assessment instruments, then we should see to it that this influence is as salutary as possible.

Taste and judgment are just as important as level and tone. The level may be demanding and the tone appropriate, but if a question doesn't help students develop a taste for mathematics or allow them to use mathematical judgment, it should be revised or replaced.

Although notions of level and tone are logically distinct from those of taste and judgment, examining test questions without attending to both sets of issues is difficult. We need to keep both sets in mind as we examine the kinds of questions now used to build mathematical assessments.

Pre-Answered Tests: A Proud Achievement of the Instant Society

If a society has a tradition of using secret examinations, it falls prey to a temptation that is often difficult to resist—the use of multiple-choice tests that can be graded automatically. It is attractive, at least in principle, to consider the prospect of widespread testing that can be done often and economically. Such testing is feasible only if the secrecy of items can be maintained, because this testing technology is built on the need for very large numbers of questions that are expensive and difficult to generate. The source of this difficulty and expense is the need to establish the validity and reliability of the questions. If the questions can be maintained in "item banks" that are not made public, then they can be used again and the cost of generating them amortized over many uses.

We can, of course, argue that the development of the technology of multiple-choice, machine-scored tests was the cause of, rather than the result of, the imposition of secrecy on the assessment process. The need to keep the contents of a test secret even after students have taken the test is probably a consequence of the economics of standardized testing. But which is cause and which is effect matters little, for currently one entails the other.

I believe that not being able to see all the items that are used to test our children has led us to accept mathematics tests and teaching that do us, individually and as a society, a profound disservice. Though we may know well the form, flavor, and feel of multiple-choice tests, the economics of large-scale, standardized testing prevents us from publicly discussing and debating the actual content of tests.

I had occasion recently to speak with an official of the Dutch Ministry of Education who was concerned with assessment of mathematics at the secondary level. He told me that the Dutch tests consist of about a dozen extended problems, each of which requires the student to understand a problem in content, to formulate an approach to the problem, to carry out that solution procedure, and finally, to explore the reasonability of the result obtained. After a test is used, it is published and enters the available body of curricular and instructional materials.[1]

Here is an example of the sort of question described, taken from the 1989 Dutch examination for secondary school students who will not pursue further studies in science or mathematics:

> The grapes in a certain vineyard are ready to be harvested. The taste of the grapes, and the wine to be made from them, is likely to be better if they are allowed to stay on the vine somewhat longer. On the other hand, the grapes could be badly damaged by heavy rains. The vineyard owner makes two analyses of the situation.
>
> I. Harvest the grapes immediately
>
> The quality of the grapes is 'reasonable.' Half the harvest can be sold for direct consumption at a price of $2.00/kilo. The other half can only be used for processing into grape juice. These grapes would bring in $1.30/kilo. In this harvesting scheme there is a limited risk.
>
> II. Harvest the grapes in two weeks' time
>
> The quality of the grapes is now 'good.' The entire harvest can be sold for $2.30/kilo. This harvesting scheme involves a greater risk. If it rains on more than 2 days in the next 2 weeks, the entire crop of grapes will only be usable for processing into grape juice at $1.30/kilo.
>
> The vineyard owner can count on a crop of 12,000 kilos.

Students are asked to consider how the risk involved in pursuing Strategy I. compares with the certainty of Strategy II. and to quantify the potential advantage and disadvantage of Strategy II. They are also asked to calculate the likelihood of rain on two or more days during the two-week period, given that the likelihood of rain on any single day in that period is 15 percent. Finally, they are asked to calculate expected outcomes for each of the strategies, to choose a strategy, and to justify their choice.

This question is reasonably structured and does not present students with an impossibly wide universe of circumstances to analyze. Moreover, it demands that students formulate and quantify such constructs as risk, advantage, and disadvantage. It also requires them to devise a procedure for calculating probabilities and expected outcomes, and to carry out those calculations.

How does the publication of examinations affect the intellectual quality of what is taught and learned in Holland? Do mathematics teachers in Holland "teach to the test"? In some senses they do, as do teachers the world over. Because tests in Holland contain problems that are rich in structure and that require students to perform a wide range of mathematical actions, mathematics instruction tends to emphasize such problems and make similar demands on students.

In the United States, educators rely on examinations that make extensive, if not exclusive, use of the multiple-choice format. What are the effects of these tests on the intellectual quality of what is taught and learned?

First, a multiple-choice item does not ask students to *produce* a solution to a problem or an answer to a question. Rather, it asks them to *recognize* a solution or an answer. Recognizing and producing are fundamentally different abilities. For example, many people have a reading knowledge of a foreign language, but have not developed the ability to speak it. Do we really want to tell students that being able to recognize the correct answer to a math question will sufficiently prepare them to use math in their everyday affairs?

Second, and even more destructive, is the implicit message that all issues worth discussing and examining can be reduced to selecting among four or five alternatives. The multiple-choice format effectively robs questions of subtlety or nuance. As a result, we are a public who believes that mathematics (and science and history and most everything else) is an intellectual domain in which questions necessarily have answers, and that these can be briefly stated. The corollary to this last point is that all questions worth asking have correct answers, which in turn implies that correct answers are unique.

Let us return, then, to the issue of the influence of tests on the level and tone of our instructional materials. If we use tests that ask students to recognize answers rather than construct solutions, we will be teaching students tricks for recognizing answers rather than strategies for constructing solutions. That is what most test preparation is now about. If we use tests that suppress subtlety and nuance, we should not be surprised that our students' analyses tend to be superficial and simplistic.

These consequences are particularly painful for mathematics in our society. Although it is true that we need people who can recognize the validity of a quantitative argument offered in support of an important public policy matter, we need more than that. We need a society of people who are as nimble using the quantitative tools of analysis as they are using the vastly subtler qualitative tools of language. We demand, and properly so, with respect to language, that the people we educate be willing and able to use their "production skills" of speaking and writing as well as their "recognition skills" of listening and reading. We can afford no less in mathematics. Assessment and, by implication, instruction that ask our students to display only recognition skills and not production skills do not serve us well.

There is yet another bitter consequence of present mathematics assessment techniques. Although mathematics, and its use in analyzing the quantitative dimensions of the world about us, is not a 'right-or-wrong' kind of enterprise, we treat it as such in our assessments. To be sure, as in most subjects, we can ask questions for which there are single correct answers. In other domains, however, we have come to understand that such questions are fundamentally trivial. History is more than dates. Literature is more than names of famous authors. And mathematics is more than 2 + 2 = 4. But mathematics assessment seems to be unable to move beyond this abysmally low level of sophistication: it's still about choosing the one correct answer.

By considering how we use mathematics in judgmental situations, we can easily see how mathematics need not be an activity with absolute, right or wrong answers. For example, we could pose a problem of this sort:

> Design the largest doghouse you can using one 8′ X 4′ sheet of plywood.

Many people might argue that students must first learn the "basics" in mathematics and that such matters as number facts, multiplication tables, and the like are not really given to interpretation. While it is true that the product of 6 and 9 has only one value, it does not follow that the only way to ascertain whether someone knows the "basics" is to ask questions like "What is the product of 6 and 9?"

For those readers whose education cheated them of the possibility of thinking about mathematics in any way except that of right or wrong answers, here are two problems that deal with the same topic, the subtraction of whole numbers:

1. What is the result of the following subtraction?

    7102
    −4595

    (a) 2493   (b) 2507   (c) 2697   (d) 2617   (e) don't know

2. Here are two subtraction problems. Make up a subtraction problem whose answer lies between the answers to the two problems that are given.[2]

    7102   6241
    −4595   −3976

These problems assess the same skill. The first has one correct answer, while the second has many correct answers (and even more incorrect ones). Moreover, the second offers the possibility of solving the problem by invoking a conceptual understanding of the meaning of subtraction that is independent of the mechanical mastery of the computational procedure. This is important because students (and even teachers) learn many computational procedures by rote without having even a glimmer of conceptual understanding.[3]

We *can* pose questions in mathematics that allow for creativity and invention. Moreover, we can do this even for those topics that are generally believed to have little room for variation. Teachers and students who know that performance will be assessed through such problems will try to develop a richer and deeper understanding of mathematics than they do now. And problems of this sort clearly can be made public with no loss of usefulness.

Secrecy: Before and After the Fact

If we are going to use assessment to constructively influence the teaching and learning of mathematics, at least two conditions must prevail. First, the assessments we use must not contradict, either explicitly or implicitly, our pedagogic goals. That is, they must not be mathematically wrong in those areas of mathematics where we want students to be mathematically right. They must not be simplistic where we want students to discern and deal with complexity. They must not convey, as they now do, an image of mathematics that is at odds with the nature of the discipline.

The second condition is that the test questions must be, at a minimum, mathematically interesting. I would accept as an educational axiom the proposition that questions with more than one correct answer are inherently more interesting than those with only one correct answer. Moreover, I believe that any question that has a single right answer can be replaced by a question with a set of correct answers that probes the same mathematical skills and is more interesting and affords greater insight into the diversity of strategies that students use in solving problems.

Suppose we succeed in altering the nature of the assessment instruments we use so that these two conditions are met. How might we then best use the tests to influence intellectuality and teaching and learning in the schools?

Making high-quality assessment items widely and easily available is one step in augmenting possible salutary intellectual effects. In this way, a wide variety of interested audiences, such as teachers, students, parents, school boards, state authorities, colleges and universities, and industrial and commercial organizations interested in hiring young people, can readily see what is expected. And widespread public availability of assessment instruments makes possible a continuing public discussion of standards by these various interested audiences, a process that can only benefit the educational system.

So far we have been talking about publishing tests after they have been administered. If the tests are good ones, then doing so can have desirable effects on what is taught and what is learned in schools. But the question of how to avoid errors in forming problems and their solutions would remain unanswered. Errors almost always will, in time, be detected after the tests are published, but that is too late.

I suggest a procedure that addresses the problem of error while preserving the potentially useful effects of assessment on instruction. Suppose that we publish past examinations, thus making a large collection of very good problems available to anyone who was interested in them. Clearly, at some point the collection becomes large enough so that problems that have been used before can be used once again. Is moving from after-the-fact open examinations to before-the-fact open examinations workable? Suffice it to say that the widespread availability of microcomputers and the easily manipulated data-base software for these machines make possible new approaches to filing, indexing, and retrieving previously used problems.

Publicly available, richly indexed data bases of problems and projects can have the kinds of salutary effects on intellectuality that we discussed above. They also provide the opportunity for scrutiny, discussion, and debate about the quality and correctness of questions and answers. From a methodological perspective, they alter completely the traditional psychometric questions of reliability and validity.

These new approaches offer the promise of an openness that we have not seen before in education. Although such openness is not in and of itself sufficient to repair the ills of mathematics education in our country, it at least establishes some conditions that are necessary for reform.

Notes

[1]Making examinations publicly available after they have been administered is not unknown in the United States. The New York State Regents' examinations are regularly published in their entirety. Generations of students and teachers in New York have used these published tests as curricular materials.

There are also "truth-in-testing" laws in several states that require testing companies to make available to test-takers, for a fee, the questions and answers of the test they have taken. These laws have not produced an avalanche of test-takers eager to see what the testers were and were not asking and what they said the answers were. It would be wrong to infer from this example, however, that publishing tests is of little value. The Regents' example shows otherwise.

[2]To solve this problem without actually carrying out the subtractions, construct a string of equivalent subtractions. For example: 7102–4595; 6102–3595; 6202– 3595; 6242–3735; 6241–3734. Thus, the first of the original problems, 7102–4595, is equivalent to the problem 6241–3734. Compare this new problem with the second of the original problems, 6241–3976. Even if we limit ourselves to integers, we can write more than 200 problems that correctly answer the question.

[3]The most notorious of the rote procedures that are ill understood by students (and by some teachers) are long division and division of fractions. The computation of logarithms and the procedure for extracting square roots, now almost never taught, were rarely understood.

9

We Must Take Care: Fitting Assessments to Functions

Walt Haney

The United States has recently witnessed numerous proposals for new nationwide examinations. The one most widely publicized came in April 1991, when President Bush announced his America 2000 strategy for educational reform (Miller 1991), which calls for new "American Achievement Tests" covering the "core subjects" of English, mathematics, science, history, and geography and based on "new world standards." This nationwide examination system "is intended to foster good teaching and learning as well as to monitor student progress. . . . Colleges will be urged to use the American Achievement Tests in admissions; [and] employers will be urged to pay attention to them in hiring" (U.S. Department of Education 1991, p. 11). The new tests are also intended to be used at the national level to help check progress toward the National Educational Goals for the Year 2000 developed by President Bush and the National Governors Association in 1990.

In announcing the America 2000 plan, President Bush said he would like the first tests available by September 1993 (Miller 1991, p. 26). Because they probably cannot be developed that quickly, the Department of Education will ask Congress to authorize the rapid deployment of individual versions of tests used by the existing National Assessment of Educational Progress, at least in reading, writing, and mathematics. If the new tests are used to monitor progress toward the 1990 National Education Goals, the tests will likely be for grades 4, 8,

Author's note: Preparation of this paper has been supported in part by a grant from the Ford Foundation. Also I would like to express my appreciation and debt to colleagues at the Center for the Study of Testing, Evaluation and Educational Policy at Boston College, and particularly the Center's director, George Madaus, for stimulation in developing ideas regarding educationally useful forms of testing and assessment.

142

and 12, since those are the levels at which the Goals call for demonstrated competency in challenging subject matter including English, mathematics, science, history and geography" (U.S. Department of Education 1991, p. 9)

The basic rationale behind this "scramble for a national test" was summed up in a recent review:

> Advocates of national testing agree that the stakes in the current system of assessment are not high enough. They believe that the only way to motivate students and schools to improve is to provide them with feedback about where they rank according to objective, national standards. Underlying the rhetoric is a kick-in-the-pants approach (Wells 1991, p. 54).

The idea that new tests may help significantly to improve our nation's schools and student learning deserves scrutiny, but what the proponents of America 2000 have not seriously considered is the importance of fitting assessments to functions. In this chapter, I briefly describe why a new national test—or a set of tests like those proposed—cannot adequately serve the range of functions set out in the America 2000 proposal for new national achievement tests.[1] Then I describe the characteristics needed in assessments aimed at serving three particular functions, namely those of school-level accountability, instructional improvement, and increased student learning. Finally, I suggest more careful strategies by which assessment for such different functions might be coordinated.

President Bush and his Secretary of Education, Lamar Alexander (who, according to press accounts, is the primary author of the new strategy), have maintained that new exams should be used to promote good teaching and learning, to hold schools and school systems accountable, to determine college admissions, and to make hiring decisions. The notion that one test or even one set of tests can do all these things evidences considerable ignorance of the evolution of testing, violates professional and legal standards concerning educational and employment testing, and defies even simple logic.

We currently use different tests for program evaluation, for college admissions, and for employment hiring simply because tests for very different purposes need very different characteristics. Professional standards regarding testing, such as those of the American Educational Research Association, the American Psychological Association, and the National Council on Measurement in Education (1985), prescribe that tests cannot be validated in the abstract but instead must be validated for their intended uses. Similarly, the Uniform Guidelines on Employment Selection Procedures (Equal Employment Opportunity Commission 1985), recognized in numerous U.S. Supreme Court decisions, prescribe that employers must validate their employment tests in terms of their relevance to the job for which people are being selected. Employers might naturally wonder why they should use the new American Achievement Tests for making hiring decisions—since for nearly three decades the federal government has told them they must validate employment tests for the particular jobs for which they are hiring.

Even if we put aside technical issues relating to test validation and the history of federal regulation of employment testing, common sense tells us that a single test cannot do all these things. If I am a student and want to learn as a result of taking a math test, I need to know exactly which problems I got wrong and why. But for the purposes of school accountability, college admissions, or employment, such detailed information is largely worthless; these purposes require summary information of quite different sorts. In short, trying to use one test for such a range of purposes is rather like trying to use one tool—say a screwdriver or a hammer—for jobs ranging from brain surgery to pile driving.

What, then, are some of the characteristics needed in assessments that serve different purposes? Discussing the whole range of purposes intended to be served by different kinds of tests—from determining school "readiness" to ascertaining suitability for job promotion—would require more space than I have here; instead I focus on three purposes that are often ascribed to tests and assessments and that are directly set out in the America 2000 proposal for the new American Achievement Tests. These are: (1) providing information for the purpose of accounting to people outside of schools, (2) providing information to teachers to help them improve instruction, and (3) helping students learn.

Ensuring School Accountability

School accountability is one of the most frequently discussed purposes of testing. Indeed, in America 2000 the proposal for the new American Achievement Tests is part of a "15-point accountability package" through which "parents, schools and communities can all be encouraged to measure results, compare results and insist on change when the results aren't good enough" (U.S. Department of Education

1991, p. 11). Yet accountability is one of the least important functions of testing and assessment.

There are two broad reasons for this general conclusion. First, schools are already held accountable in myriad ways to many audiences. They account to parents via report cards and parent-teacher meetings. They account to the school boards who oversee them. They also account to state officials (e.g., regarding student attendance) and comply with numerous state regulations (e.g., regarding the length of the school day and the duration of the school year). Schools must comply with various federal regulations if they receive federal money via categorical programs (such as Chapter 1 funds) and they report on the efficacy of their expenditures. Most schools also are subjected to scrutiny, even if irregularly, by the popular press and by numerous interest groups, such as those who are for or against religion, the theory of evolution, sex education, or cultural pluralism.

In short, despite the rhetoric about the need for more school accountability, schools are already held more accountable to many parties on many grounds than are most other social institutions. Even the America 2000 report seems to acknowledge that schools are constrained by too many requirements and regulations when it says: "The individual school is education's key action-and-accountability unit. The surest way to reform education is to give schools and their leaders the freedom and authority to make important decisions about what happens . . . " (U.S. Department of Education 1991, p. 27).

At the same time, however, many proponents of greater school accountability argue that schools have too often been held accountable by the wrong standards, for instance, by procedural requirements and financial regulations. Instead, they say, schools now must be held accountable for performance. Thus, it is not surprising that the passage quoted above ends: " . . . while being held accountable for making well-conceived efforts at improvement and for achieving desired results" (U.S. Department of Education 1991, p. 27).

In his new book, *We Must Take Charge: Schools and Our Future*, Chester Finn (1991) illustrates this view of accountability when he argues that holding schools accountable for outcomes "is the only kind of accountability worth having in 1991" (p. 149). The problem is that test results cover only a small part of the range of results for which most people think schools should be held accountable. Even the National Education Goals established by President Bush and the nation's governors in 1990 (and out of which the America 2000 strategy evolved) note this. For while two of the six goals pertain to student learning—goal 3, which says that students should have demonstrated competence in challenging subject matter, and goal 4, which says that U.S. students should be first in the world in science and math—goals 2 and 6 clearly suggest other standards by which schools should be held to account:

> Goal 2: By the year 2000, the high school graduation rate will increase to at least 90 percent.
>
> Goal 6: By the year 2000, every school in America will be free of drugs and violence and will offer a disciplined environment conducive to learning (National Education Goals Panel 1991).

Public opinion polls indicate that when it comes to assessing school quality, such school characteristics concern people more than test scores. For example, when people across the nation were asked how they rated the six national educational goals, they gave highest priority to the last goal: to free every school from drugs and violence and offer a disciplined learning environment (Elam 1990, p. 42). Similarly, when asked what aspects of a school would be most influential in their decision about where to send their children to school (should parental choice of school be adopted in their community), respondents gave substantially higher priority to the quality of the teaching staff, school discipline, curriculum, and size of classes (rated as "very important" by 87, 78, 73, and 56 percent of the national sample) than to "grades or test scores of the student body" (which was rated as "very important" by 48 percent of the sample; Elam 1990, p. 44).[2]

Thus the second reason for thinking that holding schools accountable in terms of test scores is not a terribly important function of assessment is that there are other important standards by which people judge schools. Students' test scores (or assessment results) simply cannot be used to illuminate these other standards. Indeed, some research indicates that testing programs may work against some other goals; for example, student competency testing programs may spur dropouts from school (Kreitzer, Madaus, and Haney 1989). Moreover, considerable research suggests that group-average test scores may present a very inaccurate picture of the extent to which schools or school systems are educating students. One reason for this is that group averages on tests tend to be higher when larger proportions of students are excluded from school or from testing. Thus the states with the highest college admissions test scores tend to be those where smaller proportions of students take college admissions tests (Powell and Steelman 1984). Similarly, the countries that rank higher in international test comparisons tend to be those that educate smaller proportions of their students at higher grade levels. (Rotberg 1990, 1991; see also Bradburn, Haertel, Schwille, and Torney-Purta 1991).

A second limitation with group-average test scores as indicators of school quality is that simple comparisons of school-average test scores can be highly misleading. Such averages are not only related to the socioeconomic backgrounds of students attending different schools, but are also affected by the level of learning of schools' incoming students, the extent to which teaching matches the content of the test, and schools' grade retention policies. One review of such complications offered the following advice:

> The only valid way in which assessment systems can be used to compare schools, and make inferences about a school's effectiveness, is to use longitudinal achievement data, with other variables known to affect achievement adequately represented in the analysis, and with student outcome measures that are systemically valid. Much hard work remains to be done before these goals can be realized. Meanwhile . . . assessment systems should not be reporting school comparisons. That may do more harm than good (Cooley and Bernauer 1991, pp. 168-169).[3]

Impatient education reformers doubtless view such cautions as minor and temporary technicalities or dismiss them as academic nitpicking. But even if we put aside as a minor technicality the fact that school-average test scores have been shown to be highly unreliable indices of school's effectiveness, it is worth inquiring further into the characteristics of assessments needed for the purposes of school accountability.

First, people outside the schools generally want only summary information. They want to know how schools are doing in general, not every day or week, but maybe annually or semiannually. Corporations, after all, account to their shareholders only via annual reports and annual meetings, and they typically report only quarterly to financial analysts. Similarly, school outsiders likely do not want detailed information on how every student scores in every subject, but instead want information on how students perform in basic academic areas, such as English and math. This is an important reason why standardized tests, such as college admissions tests and achievement batteries like the California, Iowa, and Metropolitan achievement tests, have never been keyed to the curriculums of particular schools, but instead to broad and commonly studied subject areas like reading comprehension and math computations. Thus, for the purposes of accountability, people generally want to know not just how a school performs in terms of that school's particular curriculum, but how it compares with similar schools in broad curriculum areas such as English and math.

Improving Instruction

Even brief reflection tells us that the kind of test results that might help teachers improve instruction have characteristics very different from those sketched above. Before discussing this point, however, let's briefly summarize evidence on the question of just how useful teachers have found standardized test results to be.

Since mid-century there have been several studies of how tests are actually used in schools (see Haney 1984 and Madaus and Kellaghan 1990, for summaries of much of this literature). Several themes emerge from these studies. First, teachers and school administrators typically know very little about the technology of testing; for instance, they often misinterpret reported scores, such as grade equivalents. Second, they view run-of-the-mill testing programs that have no clear consequences as not very useful. Salmon-Cox (1981) reported that "teachers desire diagnostic tests that are precise, closely matched to curricula and instruction, and timely. Achievement tests of the kind now widely used do not match these criteria" (p. 634). Additionally, a variety of research indicates that standardized test results do not tell teachers anything they did not already know about their students because teachers' ratings of students, independent of test scores, correspond substantially with how students perform on standardized tests (Archer 1979; Pedulla, Airasian, and Madaus 1980; Kellaghan, Madaus, and Airasian 1982; Hopkins, George, and Williams 1985).

There are two circumstances, however, under which teachers' instructional behavior is affected by students' test results. One is before a teacher has become acquainted with a student (Raudenbush 1984). A teacher has few, if any, other sources of information about a new student, so knowledge of a student's standardized test results may affect his teaching.

The other circumstance is when large consequences—for students, teachers, or schools—are attached to test results. This "high-stakes testing" often pushes teachers to focus instruction on the content and form of the important test—to "teach to the test" (Hastings, Runkel, Damrin, Kane, and Larsen 1960; Popham, Cruse, Rankin, Sandifer, and

Williams 1985; Rafferty 1985; Madaus 1988). If the stakes are high enough, some teachers and administrators will go so far as to cheat on tests (Radwin 1981, Cannell 1989).[4]

Teach to the test is exactly what some people think schools should do. James Popham (1983), for example, has long advocated "measurement-driven" instruction—that is, teaching and learning "driven" by tests. Many people, however, doubt the wisdom of this strategy. The College Board has long expressed reservations about whether the design and content of college admissions tests should influence the high school curriculum (Valentine 1987). More recently, a national survey indicated that 75 percent of teachers report that their school district's curriculum has been changed "somewhat" or "very much" to match the norm-referenced tests used in their district—and 49 percent say that curriculums have been changed to match particular questions on the tests (Hall and Kleine 1989). Forty-five percent of responding teachers said that norm-referenced tests have too much influence on what is taught in school.

There are good reasons for such reservations. By design, norm-referenced tests are intended *not* to represent a curriculum, but simply to sample skills that are included in a variety of common curriculums. Thus, when externally mandated tests "drive" instruction, both teaching and learning can suffer. A recent study of the effects of testing on elementary school teaching, for example, concludes:

> If science, civics, or critical thinking is sifted out of the curriculum because it is not tested and if exploration, discovery, integration methods fall out of use because they do not conform to the format of the mandated test, teachers will lose their capacities to teach those subjects, use these methods or even to imagine them as possibilities (Smith 1991, p. 11).

Here is how one junior high school teacher in another study expresses the problem:

> Because of the standardized test, I have found that my creativity and flexibility as a teacher have been greatly reduced. I spend a great deal of time zeroing in on skills that I know are on the test. This leaves only a bare minimum of opportunity to explore writing and enrichment reading. In reviewing the test I find that what I am going over is the same thing that teachers in one grade lower and one grade higher are covering as well. This makes for a very redundant curriculum. Also, the skills we emphasize before the tests do not help them perform better on a day-to-day basis (Haas, Haladyna, and Nolen 1990, p. 12).

Another clear problem arising from test-driven instruction is that it tends to invalidate test results. This problem became increasingly evident in the 1980s after an enterprising physician named John Cannell (1987, 1989), showed that almost all states and most school districts scored "above average" on nationally normed standardized tests. This seemingly impossible situation caused widespread consternation. One of the most widely fingered suspects behind this "Lake Wobegon" phenomenon was the practice of teaching directly to the nationally normed tests. Because the tests had been normed on national samples of schools whose instruction was not "driven" by the tests, the results for schools whose instruction was shaped by particular tests were simply not comparable with the national norm results.

The problem of invalidation of test results when instruction focuses specifically on boosting scores on a particular test was shown even more clearly in a study reported by Koretz, Linn, Dunbar, and Shepard (1991). These investigators compared the results of a high-stakes test used for several years in a large urban school district with the results of a comparable test that had not been used in that district for several years. They found that performance on the regularly used high-stakes test did not generalize to other tests for which students had not been specifically prepared. "Students in this district are prepared for high-stakes testing in ways that boost scores on that specific test substantially more than actual achievement in domains that the tests are intended to measure" (Koretz et al. 1991, p. 2). To put the matter more bluntly, teaching to a particular test invalidates the test results as indicators of more general learning.

There are considerable differences of opinion, even among proponents of new national tests, on the appropriate connection between tests and the curriculum. An addendum to the America 2000 report provides the following answer to the question of whether "national tests mean a national curriculum":

> No. . . . The American Achievement Tests will examine the *results* of education. They have nothing to say about how those results are produced, what teachers do in class from one day to the next, what instructional materials are chosen, what lesson plans are followed. They should result in *less* regulation of the means of education— because they focus exclusively on the ends (U.S. Department of Education 1991, p. 32, italics in original).

Even though on most other points Chester Finn and America 2000 agree (in fact, the Secretary of Education has publicly credited Finn's influence on his thinking), Finn forthrightly says, "Let's reject those old bugaboos that a national curriculum is a prescription for disaster and national exams are a plot to turn us into a land of dutiful robots. . . . I visualize a *nationwide* core curriculum matched to the education goals set by the president and governors in 1990" (Finn 1991, p. 247). According to the evidence available on high-stakes testing, Finn is clearly correct in recognizing that when important sanctions are attached to test results, the test comes to define the curriculum in terms of both what gets taught and how it gets taught. If we are going to have a high-stakes national test, disclaimers of America 2000 notwithstanding, then we are de facto also going to have a national curriculum.

But Finn is also mistaken when he argues that though the core ends of education need to be commonly defined nationwide and communicated through national standards and tests, "*the means by which we reach those ends are the province of expert professionals*" and "we should *revitalize the delivery system by vesting management authority and responsibility in building level educators*" (Finn 1991, p. 246, italics in original). He is wrong precisely because whenever strong sanctions are attached to test results (and school accountability, college admissions, and employment opportunities would be an unprecedentedly wide range of important sanctions to attach to a single test), teachers will teach not just to the content but also to the form, of the test. As Smith (1991) concludes in her study of the effects of external mandated testing programs on elementary teachers:

> A teacher who is able to teach only that which is determined from above and can teach only from worksheets is an unskilled worker. Far from the reflective practitioner or the empowered teacher, those optimistic images of the 1980s, the image we project of teachers in the world after testing reform is that of interchangeable technicians receiving the standard curriculum from above, transmitting it as given (the presentation manual never leaving the crook of their arms), and correcting multiple-choice responses of their pupils (p. 11).

Thus it is either extremely naive—or entirely disingenuous—for Alexander and Finn to say that we are going to create new national tests in five subjects to be used for evaluating learning at grades 4, 8, and 12, *and* for holding schools accountable *and* for regulating college admissions and employment opportunities, but then to maintain that we are also going to give schools and their leaders more "freedom and authority to make important decisions about what happens" (U.S. Department of Education 1991). Sorry, Mr. Alexander and Mr. Finn, we simply cannot have it both ways.

For the moment, though, let's put aside the fact that Alexander and Finn's kick-em-in-the-pants-with-a-tough-national-test approach is inconsistent with the aim of giving schools and their leaders more freedom and professional authority to make important decisions, and summarize briefly some of the characteristics of assessments that help teachers improve their teaching. Clearly teachers do not need information about how their school ranks against some other school; they need information about how their own students perform. In some cases—for instance, in planning a review lesson for a whole class—teachers may want to identify common problems; they need information about patterns of performance among all their students. In many instances, however—maybe to help Johnny over the hump of solving quadratic equations—they want information on individual students' performance. In other words, teachers want assessments that provide them with diagnostic information to help identify strengths and weaknesses in particular students and among groups of students in individual classes and in particular subjects. Also, given that teachers teach every day, they want rapid feedback, if not within minutes, then at least within a day or two. This desideratum is generally inconsistent with external testing programs (i.e., testing programs created outside individual schools) in which tests are sent away to be scored by machines or by independent raters.

Finally, teachers want tests and assessments that are integrated with teaching and learning. Instead of taking time away from teaching, such tests might be "embedded" within teaching and learning activities that are already part of a class. Ironically, this is exactly the approach called for in a federally sponsored report on testing, teaching, and learning that preceded America 2000 by a dozen years:

> Instructional guidance is the educational activity which is least served by existing tests. Yet the interaction between teacher and pupil is at the heart of school. Further, use of tests for purposes outside the classroom —accountability, selection, evaluation—should come out of classroom process, not be imposed on it like a foreign body (Tyler and White 1979, p. 22).

Helping Students Learn

People often claim that tests help students learn, but they rarely consider in detail exactly how they do so. The theory implicit in America 2000 appears to be that if we kick students hard enough with tough national tests, they will be motivated to learn more. This "theory" is elaborated on by Finn (1991), who devotes one section of his book to discussing the merits of internal versus external incentives for increasing student learning. Asking whether we can ever really expect to make algebra more seductive than television, or chemistry more beguiling than rock music, he implicitly answers his own question by writing: "When it comes to academic learning, I believe that external consequences are the main determinant of how hard we work" (Finn 1991, p. 125).

The problem with this theory as a strategy for school reform is that, apart from the sort of anecdotal evidence provided by Finn (he quotes a science teacher bemoaning the decline of the work ethic among students), there appears to be little evidence that lack of motivation to do well in school is a key problem in students' learning. One major study of motivation and student effort in a large urban school district, for example, concluded:

> Students in our studies reported that evaluations of their performance in school were central to their life interests. . . . Evaluations of performance were seen as affecting important material sanctions in the future, in the form of jobs and careers, as well as important social sanctions in the present in the form of the opinions of parents, counselors, and friends. Moreover these sanctions were considered as very important by most students. . . .
>
> Low-achieving students, as well as minority group students, were just as likely as high-achieving students and Anglo students to report that evaluations received in school were influential. Since most students in our studies perceived evaluations of their school performance as being influential, low student effort and low achievement in school cannot be attributed to lack of influential evaluations (Natriello and Dornbush 1984, pp. 137-138).

Thus, the "theory" that new national tests will increase student learning by attaching higher stakes to test results appears to be based on a faulty premise. If we cannot attribute low achievement to a current lack of influential evaluations, how will more influential evaluations via national tests and external sanctions possibly improve matters?

Another problem with this kick-em-in-the-pants theory of motivation is that some research indicates extensive testing may actually contribute to increasing student disillusionment and decreasing motivation. For instance, in a survey of students in grades 2 through 11 in four large states, Paris, Lawton, Turner, and Roth (1991) found "negative impact [of testing] on students that can be summarized in three general trends: growing disillusionment about tests, decreasing

motivation to give genuine effort [on tests], and increasing use of
inappropriate strategies" (p. 14). Moreover, in a second survey in another
state, the same investigators found that

> the results of standardized tests become increasingly less valid for low
> achievers, exactly the group who are most at risk for educational
> problems and who most need diagnostic testing. Their scores may be
> contaminated by inappropriate motivation and learning strategies that
> further debilitate their performance and affirm a self-fulfilling
> prophecy of low scores. Apparently in their efforts to decrease personal
> anxiety and increase the protection of their own self-esteem, they
> relinquish effort and appropriate strategies on standardized
> achievement tests (Paris et al. 1991, p. 16).

Since testing does not seem to improve student learning indirectly
via motivation, perhaps we should consider how tests might aid student
learning more directly—a matter that is rarely considered seriously with
regard to external tests. Though much standardized testing is often
described as "educational," the features that facilitate student learning are
so notably lacking that the term "educational testing" is at present mainly
a malapropism in terms of helping test takers learn (Haney 1985).

Let's consider some of the essential elements needed to help
someone learn. If I'm trying to learn something new, I need to be able to
practice it. To learn from an experience, I need rapid and detailed
feedback on the results. This feedback doesn't have to come from an
external authority like a teacher (much less a national commission or
testing agency); surely one aim of education and child-rearing generally
is that people become autonomous and self-regulating adults, capable of
judging the success of their own endeavors, rather than attending forever
to external sanctions and the judgments of foreign authorities.

Consider, for example, the learning of skill in sports. If I want to
learn how to shoot free throws in basketball, all I need to do is try and
the results are immediately obvious. What I need is ongoing feedback, in
context, as I try to improve my performance: I need to know whether my
shots went through the hoop, not whether my shooting meets someone
else's standard of satisfactory free-throw shooting.

This example is instructive, for my free-throw shooting is pretty
lousy. Most certainly it does not meet "world-class" standards—indeed it
does not meet the standards of the local elementary school's 6th grade
team. But if I want to learn the skill of free-throw shooting, I need
practice and an opportunity to see how well my various attempts

succeed, not a formal assessment of basketball skills based on someone else's standards.

Similar necessary conditions for promoting learning have been recognized for many decades in many theories of learning—for instance in Edward Thorndike's (1913) law of effect, which holds essentially that learning is enhanced when people see effects from what they try. Researchers have also identified conditions conducive to learning. Malone (1980), in his study of what makes for intrinsically motivating educational computer games, found, for instance, that attributes such as rapid feedback, variable difficulty so as to provide appropriate challenge, and randomness in presentation features of games contribute to learning motivation. More recently, a meta-analysis of forty previous studies on the instructional effects of feedback in test-like events showed that relatively rapid feedback (i.e., immediately after a test was completed) is more effective than feedback given a day or more after a test. Also, feedback providing guidance to, or identification of, correct answers is more instructionally effective than feedback that simply tells learners whether their answers are right or wrong (Bangert-Drowns, Kulik, Kulik, and Morgan 1991).

Common sense, theories of learning, and research on intrinsic motivation and on instructional feedback—all of these clearly indicate that the sort of standardized testing now commonly employed in schools and via which students do not get rapid or specific feedback on their work, but only summary scores after days, if not weeks, of delay, is simply not conducive to student learning.

Fitting Assessments

Some proponents of new national tests have argued that testing problems in American schools derive mainly from the form of the tests. Most tests used today are mainly multiple-choice, and many people argue that they emphasize memorization and "lower-order" thinking skills. During the 1980s, increased pressure on students, teachers, and schools to raise test scores drove "teachers to emphasize tasks that would reinforce rote learning and sharpen test-taking skills, and discouraged curricula that promote complex thinking and active learning" (Wells 1991, p. 55). Indeed, in 1984 one testing specialist argued that the influence of multiple-choice testing on teaching and learning was the "real" source of bias in tests (Frederiksen 1984).

Proponents of new national tests generally are calling for new forms of assessment, which they call "authentic" or "instructionally worthy" assessments. What people mean by this term varies, but the most commonly discussed kinds of alternatives to multiple-choice tests are portfolios of student work and performance assessments in which students perform a task or solve an open-ended problem. Probably the most common "performance assessment" is the essay test, and there is some evidence that teachers do find essay tests more instructionally useful than multiple-choice tests of writing skills (Suhor 1985).

I won't go into detail on the pros and cons of different kinds of assessment and their feasibility and validity for different purposes. It is worth noting, however, that many of the kinds of assessments being touted as new alternatives to multiple-choice tests are not at all new and that considerable evidence casts doubt on recent hopes and claims regarding their utility as external examinations (Haney and Madaus 1989).[5]

This does not mean we ought not pursue inquiry into alternative forms of educational assessment. As the National Commission on Testing and Public Policy states:

> Testing programs should be redirected from over-reliance on multiple-choice tests toward alternative forms of assessment. . . .
>
> A major cause for the distortion of test results and the ill effects of testing over the last several decades has been that the same test, or kind of test, has been asked to serve many important but different functions. Therefore, we recommend that testing for different purposes be differentiated and disentangled. Specifically, we urge that assessment of the effectiveness of social institutions—such as schools and training programs—be differentiated from assessment of individuals in order to help them (NCTPP 1990, pp. 26, 30).

Testing and assessment for the purposes of improving teaching and learning within schools obviously need to be coordinated with external testing programs aimed at school accountability. But if we are serious about schools being "education's key action and accountability unit" and about preventing the form of assessment from dictating the manner of teaching and learning, we ought to employ sampling techniques that focus on schools as the entities about which accountability information is to be gathered—and such accountability information ought not be limited to test or assessment results.

It is inefficient to have all students in a school spend all the time available for assessment answering traditional multiple-choice test questions or undergoing any other one form of assessment. School-level accountability or "quality control" can be more efficiently realized by using matrix sampling techniques to select samples of grade levels and samples of students within grades, and then to employ a wider range of outcome measures across the different samples. Even the America 2000 report implicitly recognizes the value of sampling, for it calls for American Achievement Tests for just grades 4, 8, and 12. But the sampling implicitly called for in America 2000 is, from both a scientific and organizational point of view, *very* inefficient. Sampling just grade 4 of the six elementary grades, for instance, tells us little, from a statistical inference point of view, about other grades; and from an organizational point of view, it clearly keeps the accountability boot off the pants of grade 5 and 6 teachers.

If we are serious about assessment for school accountability, we need to employ matrix sampling techniques that systematically sample grades, students, and forms of assessment. Although the details of such matrix sampling would have to be worked out differently in different schools, let's use as an example a school with four grades and 100 students in each grade. If a random sample of twenty-five students in one grade were given one set of assessments, we could be 95 percent confident that the sample's performance on that set will represent very closely the performance of all students in that grade had they all been given the same set of assessments. The other three-quarters of each grade could be given different sets of assessments, resulting in a sixteen-fold increase in information about school quality as compared with the America 2000 approach of testing all students in just one grade with the same test.

Systematic matrix sampling would permit the use of a wider range of assessment techniques than if all students were tested with the same instrument. Judicious use of samples has long been recognized in quality-control procedures in accounting, business, and industry. General Motors may want to crash-test its cars and check the durability of its paint finishes. Obviously, though, it does not conduct such tests on all cars coming off the assembly line or even conduct both tests on the same cars. In their advocacy of one test or one set of tests for all students and all purposes, proponents of new national tests largely ignore this point.[6]

From an educational point of view, such sampling would also have benefits. First, it would substantially decrease the burden of external testing or assessment on schools, as compared with giving all students all relevant forms of assessments. And perhaps more important, by focusing on the *school* as the unit of accountability and giving equal chance for any teacher's students to be assessed on any of, say, four forms of assessment (maybe essays, open-ended problem solving, portfolio review, and multiple-choice questions), teachers would be freed from the need to model their teaching on one form of assessment.

This is vital, for as Finn (1991, p. 168) notes, alternative kinds of assessments are "at least as vulnerable to manipulation" as multiple-choice tests. As clear evidence that performance assessments will not solve the problem of the corruption of high-stakes accountability testing, we need only be reminded of the "payment-by-results" scheme used in England in the 19th century.

In May 1862, the English parliament passed the Revised Code under which schools would be paid not just on the basis of student attendance, but also on the basis of "results of the examination of individual children" by school inspectors (Connell 1950, p. 205). The main sentiments behind the payment-by-results plan appear to have been remarkably similar to those now motivating the current scramble in the United States for new national accountability tests. One backer of the Revised Code told his colleagues in Parliament that it would allow the public "to know exactly what consideration they get for their money." He continued:

> I cannot promise the House that this system [payment by results] will be an economical one, and I cannot promise that it will be an efficient one, but I can promise that it will be one or the other. If it is not cheap, it shall be efficient; if it is not efficient it shall be cheap (quoted in Connell 1950, p. 207).

The examinations to determine school payments were entirely "performance-based"—actual reading from a schoolbook, newspaper, or modern narrative; writing from dictation; and solving open-ended arithmetic problems. They were to stress the ability of pupils to exercise skills "in such a manner as will really enable them to employ those attainments in the practical business of life" (Connell 1950, p. 210).

The payment-by-results scheme was much debated and was revised in the 1870s and 1880s (in part to provide additional payments for students passing examinations in specialized subjects such as history and geography, or what now would likely be called higher-order skills and knowledge). Finally, in 1890 the payment-by-results plan was abandoned altogether.[7]

Though a full story of the payment-by-results scheme cannot be told here,[8] suffice it to say that the main reasons for its demise appear to have been the administrative burden it imposed, the success over time of efforts to cram students for the exams (and the concomitant increases in government expenditures), the stifling of teachers and "overpressuring" of students, and ultimately the corruption of examination results. One critic likened the payment of schools by results to "the payment of gardeners for planting in or out of season, a shrubbery of evergreens for show on a special occasion, no matter of its dying off immediately after" (quoted in Sutherland 1973, p. 251).

One of the more eloquent opponents of the payment-by-results scheme was Matthew Arnold. Though at the time Arnold was a school inspector in the Education Department, he spoke out repeatedly about the ill effects of the scheme on pupils, teachers, and teacher training:

> In a country where everyone is prone to rely too much on mechanical processes, and too little on intelligence, [the Revised Code] inevitably gives a mechanical turn to the school teaching. . . . It attempts to lay down to the very letter, the requirements which shall be satisfied in order to earn grants. The teacher in consequence is led to think, not about teaching his subject, but about managing to hit those requirements (quoted in Connell 1950, p. 225).[9]

Arnold viewed schools as centers of culture and argued that their general role in civilizing pupils was far more vital than the mere teaching of skills and knowledge. He argued that the government should support a school "not as a mere machine for teaching reading writing and arithmetic, but as a living whole with complex functions, religious, moral and intellectual" (quoted in Connell 1950, pp. 213-214).[10]

* * *

I have expanded briefly on the idea of taking school-level accountability assessment seriously, and on the English experience in the last century of holding schools accountable via "performance" exams, simply as a way of showing how poorly conceived are the accountability testing schemes of America 2000. As argued previously, accountability seems to me the least important of the three functions of assessment discussed here. If the primary motivation behind the America 2000 proposal is indeed educational, in the sense that what we need—more than bigger accountability schemes and greater sanctions attached to test results—are better ways to help children learn and better ways of helping teachers and parents help them do so, then we ought to focus any time and energy devoted to assessment *directly* on those ends rather than on some pile-driving, kick-em-in-the-pants accountability scheme. As in medicine, the sort of brain surgery we should work on our children requires better and more delicate instruments, much more deftly and carefully applied, than those for driving piles—or political campaigns.

Notes

[1]Various proposals for new national tests might easily be critiqued on bases other than those set out here. Madaus and Kellaghan (1991), for example, raise numerous questions about current proposals for new national testing in the United States via an analysis of national testing systems in European Community nations. To limit the scope of this chapter, however, I focus mainly on the America 2000 proposal and the problem of trying to use one test or set of tests for different functions.

[2]Even though he cites evidence from Gallup polls in more than a half-dozen places, Finn (1991) seems to have overlooked the Gallup poll evidence summarized in this paragraph when he writes: "Most Americans are accustomed to gauging the performance of their school systems by whether those [test] scores are rising or falling" (p. 99). Though Finn seems to wish otherwise, test scores do not seem to be the primary criterion by which people judge school quality.

[3]For a similar critique of the value of school-average college admissions test scores as indicators of school quality, see Fetler 1991.

[4]Despite much recent publicity about instances of teachers' cheating on tests (including one 60 Minutes television program devoted to a South Carolina teacher who got fired for cheating), the vast majority of educational personnel responding to an anonymous national survey indicated that less than 10 percent of teachers in their school district engage in "non-standard" testing practices (Hall and Kleine 1989).

[5]Chester Finn is not a Pollyanna on alternatives to multiple-choice tests. He writes that "other kinds of tests and evaluations one would like to see given are more cumbersome, time-consuming, costly, and at least as vulnerable to manipulation. They are subject to uneven standards among those conducting and evaluating them—people rather than machines—and, to the extent that they are not administered in a controlled setting, may invite more cheating" (Finn 1991, p. 168). His gaze does seem rather rosy, however, when he continues, "I believe that this is where we'll likely see the greatest payoff from the R&D now under way."

[6]Finn is a bit ambiguous on the potential value of such sampling strategies. At one point he suggests that when checking on the performance of schools or states "data can easily (and economically) be generated by a test administered to a statistical sample of the larger population involved" (Finn 1991, pp. 166-167). Later, in an outburst of enthusiasm for "outcomes" accountability, he seems to gloss over this earlier remarks on the possibility of different kinds of assessments for different purposes when he writes: "at every level of the education system (child, classroom, school building, locality, state and nation) we must demand a steady flow of reliable information about student achievement and other important outcomes. . . . Mr. and Mrs. Brady have to know how Janet and Jerome are doing in school, how their school is performing, and how their state is faring. This information needs to include comparisons with national standards and international performance levels that are clear and intelligible to laymen" (pp. 248-249, italics in original).

[7]Payment by results started later and lasted longer in Ireland than in England, but appears to have had many of the same effects on schools (Madaus, Ryan, Kellaghan, and Airasian 1987).

⁸For a short but very useful account, see Rapple 1990; Sutherland (1973) provides a broader account that shows the complexity of the political considerations surrounding payment by results.

⁹Ironically, though Finn (1991) argues that "every young person deserves a full measure of what Matthew Arnold termed 'the best which has been though and said,' as well as real math, authentic science and engaging history" (p. 253), he seems unaware of Arnold's opposition, not to examinations of individual pupils, but to the payment-by-results scheme of holding schools accountable in terms of pupils' performance on exams.

¹⁰For more on Arnold, see Connell 1950.

References

American Educational Research Association, American Psychological Association, and National Council on Measurement and Education. (1985). *Standards for Educational and Psychological Testing.* Washington D.C.: American Psychological Association.

Archer, P. (1979). *A Comparison of Teacher Judgements of Pupils and the Results of Standardized Tests.* Master's diss., University College Cork, Ireland.

Bangert-Drowns, R. L., C. C. Kulik, J. A. Kulik, and M. Morgan. (1991). "The Instructional Effect of Feedback in Test-Like Events." *Review of Educational Research* 61, 2: 213-238.

Bradburn, N., E. Haertel, J. Schwille, and J. Torney-Purta. (1991). "A Rejoinder to 'I Never Promised You First Place.'" *Phi Delta Kappan* 72, 10: 774-777.

Cannell, J. J. (1987). *Nationally Normed Elementary Achievement Testing in America's Public Schools: How all Fifty States are Above the National Average.* Daniels, W.Va.: Friends for Education.

Cannell, J. J. (1989). *The 'Lake Wobegon' Report: How Public Educators Cheat on Standardized Achievement Tests.* Albuquerque, N.M.: Friends for Education.

Connell, W. F. (1950). *The Educational Thought and Influence of Mathew Arnold.* London: Rutledge and Kegan Paul.

Cooley, W. W., and J. A. Bernauer. (1991). "School Comparisons in Statewide Testing Programs." In *Advances in Program Evaluation,* edited by R. E. Stake. Greenwich, Conn.: JAI Press.

Elam, S. M. (1990). "The 22nd Annual Gallup Poll of the Public's Attitudes Toward the Public Schools." *Phi Delta Kappan* 72, 1: 41-55.

Equal Employment Opportunity Commission, U.S. Department of Labor, Office of Personnel Management. (1985). *Uniform Guidelines on Employment Selection Procedures,* 29 CFR Part 1607. Washington, D.C.: U.S. Government Printing Office.

Fetler, M. E. (1991). "Pitfalls of Using SAT Results to Compare Schools." *American Educational Research Journal* 28, 2: 481-491.

Finn, C. E. J. (1991). *We Must Take Charge: Our Schools and Our Future.* New York: Free Press.

Frederiksen, N. (1984). "The Real Test Bias: Influence of Testing on Teaching and Learning." *American Psychologist* 39, 3: 193-202.

Haas, N. S., T. M. Haladyna, and S. B. Nolen. (April 1989) "Standardized Achievement Testing: War Stories from the Trenches." Paper presented at the Annual Meeting of the National Council on Measurement in Education, Boston.

Haladyna, T. M., S. B. Nolen, and N. S. Haas. (1991). "Raising Standardized Test Scores and the Origins of Test Score Pollution." *Educational Researcher* 20, 5: 2-7.

Hall, J. L., and P. F. Kleine. (April 1989). "Educator Perceptions of National Achivement Test Use and Abuse: A National Survey." Paper presented at the Annual Meeting of the National Council on Measurement in Education, Boston.

Haney, W. (1984). "Testing Reasoning and Reasoning About Testing." *Review of Educational Research* 54, 4: 597–654.

Haney, W. (1985). "Making Testing More Educational." *Educational Leadership* 43, 2: 4–13.

Haney, W., and G. F. Madaus. (1989). "Searching for Alternatives to Standardized Tests: Whys, Whats, and Whethers." *Phi Delta Kappan* 70, 9: 683-687.

Hastings, J., D. Damrin, P. Runkel, R. Kane, and G. Larsen. (1960). *The Use of Test Results.* Urbana: Bureau of Educational Research, University of Illinois.

Hopkins, K. D., C. A. George, and D. Williams. (1985). "The Concurrent Validity of Standardized Achievement Tests by Content Area Using Teachers' Ratings as Criteria." *Journal of Educational Measurement* 22, 3: 177-182.

Kelleghan, T., G. F. Madaus, and P. W. Airasian. (1982). *The Effects of Standardized Testing.* Boston: Kluwer-Nijhoff Publishing.

Koretz, D. M., R. L. Linn, S. B. Dunbar, and L. A. Shepard. (1991). "The Effects of High Stakes Testing on Achievement: Preliminary Findings About Generalization Across Tests." Paper presented at the Annual Meeting of the American Educational Research Association, Chicago.

Kreitzer, A., G. Madaus, and W. Haney. (1989). "Competency Testing and Dropouts." In *Dropouts from School: Issues, Dilemmas and Solutions,* edited by L. Weis, E. Farrar, and H. Petrie. Albany: State University of New York Press.

Madaus, G. F. (1988). "The Influence of Testing on the Curriculum." In *Critical Issues in Curriculum,* Eighty-seventh Yearbook of the National Society for Study of Education, edited by L. Tanner. Chicago: University of Chicago Press.

Madaus, G. F., and T. Kelleghan. (1990). "Curriculum Evaluation and Assessment." In *Handbook on Research on Curriculum,* edited by P. W. Jackson. New York: Macmillan.

Madaus, G. F., and T. Kelleghan. (1991). *Student Examination Systems in the European Community: Lessons for the United States.* (Contractor report). Washington, D.C.: Office of Technology Assessment, U.S. Congress.

Madaus, G. F., J. Ryan, T. Kelleghan, and P. W. Airasian. (1987). "Payment by Results: An Analysis of a Nineteenth Century Performance-Contracting Programme." *The Irish Journal of Education* 21, 1 and 2: 80-91.

Miller, J. A. (April 24, 1991). "Bush Strategy Launches 'Crusade' for Education." *Education Week* X, 31: 1, 26.

NCTPP. (1990). *From Gatekeeper to Gateway: Transforming Testing in America.* Chestnut Hill, Mass.: National Commission on Testing and Public Policy.

National Education Goals Panel. (1991). *Measuring Progress Toward the National Education Goals: Potential Indicators and Measurement Strategies.* Washington, D.C.: National Education Goals Panel.

Natriello, G., and S. M. Dornbush. (1984). *Teacher Evaluative Standards and Student Effort.* New York: Longman.

Paris, S. G., T. A. Lawton, J. C. Turner, and J. L. Roth. (1991). "A Developmental Perspective on Standardized Achievement Testing." *Educational Researcher* 20, 5: 12-20.

Pedulla, J. J., P. W. Airasian, and G. F. Madaus. (1980). "Do Teacher Ratings and Standardized Test Results of Students Yield the Same Information? *American Educational Research Journal* 17: 303-307.

Popham, W. J. (1983). "Measurements as an Instructional Catalyst." *New Directions for Testing and Measurement* 17: 19-30.

Popham, W. J., K. L. Cruse, S. C. Rankin, P. D. Sandifer, and P. L. Williams. (1985). "Measurement-Driven Instruction: It's on the Road." *Phi Delta Kappan* 66, 9: 628-635.

Powell, B., and L. C. Steelman. (1984). "Variations in State SAT Performance: Meaningful or Misleading?" *Harvard Educational Review* 54: 389-412.

Radwin, E. (1981). *A Case Study of New York City: Citywide Reading Testing Program.* Cambridge, Mass.: The Huron Institute.

Rafferty, M. (1985). "Examinations in Literature: Perceptions from Nontechnical Writers of England and Ireland from 1850 to 1984." Unpublished doctoral dissertation, Boston College.

Rapple, B. A. (1990). *Payment by Educational Results: An Idea Whose Time Has Gone?* Normal: Center for the Study of Educational Finance, Illinois State University.

Raudenbush, S. (1984). "Magnitude of Teacher Expectancy Effects on Pupil IQ as a Function of the Credibility of Expectancy Induction." *Journal of Educational Psychology* 76, 1: 85-91.

Rotberg, I. (December 1990). "I Never Promised You First Place." *Phi Delta Kappan* 72, 4: 296-303.

Rotberg, I. (June 1991). "How Did All Those Dumb Kids Make All Those Smart Bombs?" *Phi Delta Kappan* 72, 10: 778-781.

Salmon-Cox, L. (1981). "Teachers and Standardized Achievement Tests: What's Really Happening?" *Phi Delta Kappan* 62, 9: 631-634.

Smith, M. L. (1991). "Put to the Test: The Effects of External Testing on Teachers." *Educational Researcher* 20, 5: 8-11.

Suhor, C. (1985). "Objective Tests and Writing Samples: How Do They Affect Instruction in Composition?" *Phi Delta Kappan* 66, 9: 635-639.

Sutherland, G. (1973). *Policy-Making in Elementary Education, 1870-1895.* London: Oxford University Press.

Thorndike, E. L. (1913). *Educational Psychology, Vol. 1, The Psychology of Learning.* New York: Teachers College.

Tyler, R., and S. White. (1979). "Testing, Teaching and Learning: Report of a Conference on Research on Testing." Washington, D.C.: National Institute of Education.

U.S. Department of Education. (1991). *America 2000: An Education Strategy.* (ED/OS91-13). Washington, D.C.: U.S. Department of Education.

Valentine, J. A. (1987). *The College Board and the School Curriculum.* New York: College Entrance Examination Board.

Wells, P. (Spring 1991). "Putting America to the Test." *Agenda* 1: 52-57.

10

Toward More Powerful Assessment

Vito Perrone

The message underlying all the chapters of this book is that we must move assessment activities closer to the actual work of teachers and children; we must make classrooms the starting points for linking learning to large educational and social purposes. In *Schools of Thought* (San Francisco: Jossey-Bass, 1991), Rexford Brown argues that the most active, thoughtful learning, involving the most energized students, happens in schools that use no standardized tests. He asks: Do we want thoughtfulness in schools? Do we want learning that means something? Do we want learning that can be taken into the world?

As I consider thoughtfulness in Brown's terms, I begin with questions of purpose. To speak of large purposes within this framework means trying to instill in students not just the mechanics of reading and writing, but also a love for reading and writing. It means providing them the opportunity to *practice* democracy, not just learn *about* democratic thought. It means encouraging them to *construct* knowledge, not just hear about it. It means making sure they experience the power of cooperation and collaborative thought, not just the pressures of competition. It means developing their ability to question—to bring a healthy skepticism to the world—not just to accept fully the vested authority around them. It means encouraging *all* students to explore the aesthetic aspects of life through the arts, not just grooming a select few or accepting a view that the arts are frills, not basic enough. These kinds of purposes call out loudly for a reconsideration of the evaluation process.

To speak of large purposes is also to want our students to become *active* readers and writers—individuals who read newspapers and magazines, find beauty in a poem or love story, see Romeo and Juliet in their own lives. We want students to develop an optimistic view about the world and their place in it, to take time to really look at the trees or

164

enjoy a sunset or study the stars. We want them to participate in politics and community life, have a vision of themselves as thoughtful mothers and fathers, understand and value work in all its dimensions, and become sensitive to the needs and values of older citizens. We want them to not only be able to locate the Republic of South Africa on a map, but to understand apartheid and feel the pain associated with it. We need to find student assessments that will help us achieve rather than thwart such purposes.

On yet another level, particularly in relation to the schools themselves, considering large purposes means understanding that our students are learning all the time: that they are constantly gaining what Jean Piaget calls a balance between changing the world and changing themselves. What do our current student evaluation systems tell us about this important growth? Focusing on large purposes means beginning with students' natural strengths and energies—in this regard, fitting the schools to the students, not fitting the students to the schools. The distinction is extremely important and if followed out to its fullest conclusion would mean far less standardization of curriculum and organizational structures. The standardized tests that now exist would mean nothing. Different assessments would be an imperative. But are we prepared for such a reformulation?

To keep large purposes before us is also to acknowledge the multicultural nature of our society, to find ways of celebrating diversity and supporting the many languages that surround us. How do we respond, for example, to the fact that our students and the adults who have gone through the schools have so much difficulty talking together about matters of race, class, ethnicity, gender, and language difference? To the recent Louis Harris Poll which suggests that racial attitudes are growing more negative among young people? How do we stay close to such issues in our student evaluation systems? Does it matter?

To consider large purposes is also to fashion a more integrated curriculum, one that stresses continuities, not divisions, between disciplines, in which topics are revisited often, and grade levels and the clock do not *limit* what students learn; where students have the time needed to do work that they can honor, that helps them build a culture of high standards and high quality.

In a school that puts forward such large purposes, *understanding*, not just knowing, is the goal. What is behind the math algorithms, the metaphors, the lines of poetry, the historical periods, the geological ages, and the genetic codes would assume prominence. Instead of simply drilling children on grammatical forms, for example, teaching would be directed toward helping students develop an appreciation for language and a love of writing.

I raise these teacher, school, and pedagogical issues—abbreviated as they are—to make clear that larger conceptions of evaluation cannot go forward without a larger conception of teaching. If teaching is skill sheets, work sheets, textbooks, basal readers, and simplified explanations, a larger view of assessment is not likely to take root. Who wants, for example, a portfolio of skill sheets? We have a chance to construct something better.

The educators who contributed to this book did not, as they might have, use their space merely to criticize current methods of standardized testing; they already know that assessment needs to go beyond most current testing technologies if schools are to be powerful educational settings. Implicit in their goals is the belief that assessment should empower students as learners. In fact, the kinds of assessment activities that are *authentic*—the portfolios, documentation, and exhibitions discussed in this book, for example—contribute importantly to student self-evaluation. We often hear that students aren't interested in their own growth as learners, that they don't want responsibility for being involved in assessment practices. Yet when students have had sustained opportunities to be active participants, to review, for example, their own writing over time, they have become increasingly more articulate about their progress and what they need to work on to improve their performance and enlarge their understandings.

Many people view the movement toward authentic assessment as a difficult, enigmatic process that demands too much of teachers. But the contributors to this book believe that these different assessments benefit not only students, but teachers. Once teachers begin such efforts, the difficulties fall away and their work becomes, in a sense, easier. They become thoughtful observers, documenters, and organizers of evaluation.

In the end these fresh directions are not as complex as they appear. They call upon us to ask, in relation to purposes, what would cause us to say that our students are thinkers, readers, writers, or comprehenders of knowledge, and to then work out systematic processes to follow up such questions. In doing so, we make assessment a more powerful educational tool and return credibility to school practice. Most important, though, we improve the quality of student learning.

Contributing Authors

Vito Perrone is Director of Teacher Education and Chair of Teaching Curriculum and Learning Environments, Harvard Graduate School of Education, 224 Longfellow Hall, Appian Way, Cambridge, MA 02138.

Ron Berger is a 6th Grade Teacher at Shutesbury Elementary School, West Pellham Road, Shutesbury, MA 01702.

Edward Chittenden is a Research Psychologist at the Educational Testing Service, Rosedale Road, Princeton, NJ 08541.

Patricia Carini is the founder of Prospect Center, P.O. Box 326, North Bennington, VT 05257.

David Carroll is the Coordinator for Teacher Education and Evaluation Services, Prospect Center, P.O. Box 326, North Bennington, VT 05257.

Howard Gardner is Professor of Education and Co-Director of Harvard Project Zero, Harvard Graduate School of Education, 323 Longfellow Hall, Appian Way, Cambridge, MA 02138.

Walt Haney is Associate Professor of Education and Senior Research Associate, Center for the Study of Testing, Evaluation, and Educational Policy, Boston College, 523 McGuinn Hall, Chestnut Hill, MA 02167.

George Hein is Professor of Liberal Studies and Adult Learning Programs, Lesley College, 29 Everett St., Cambridge, MA 02138-2790.

Kathe Jervis is a Staff Associate at the Institute for Literacy Studies, Lehman College, Bedford Park Blvd. West, Bronx, NY 10468-1589.

Judah L. Schwartz is a Professor in the Educational Technology Center of the Harvard Graduate School of Education, 13 Appian Way, Cambridge, MA 02138. He also teaches in the School of Engineering at the Massachusetts Institute of Technology.

Patricia Lambert Stock is Associate Professor, Department of English, Michigan State University, Morrill Hall, East Lansing, MI 48824-1036.

Rieneke Zessoules is a Researcher at Harvard Project Zero, Harvard Graduate School of Education, 323 Longfellow Hall, Appian Way, Cambridge, MA 02138.

Current ASCD Networks on Assessment

ASCD sponsors numerous networks that help members exchange ideas, share common interests, identify and solve problems, grow professionally, and establish collegial relationships. Two may be of particular interest to readers of this book:

Authentic Assessment Network

Contact: Albert Koshiyama, Administrator, School Intervention, California Department of Education, 502 J Street, Sacramento, CA 95814. Telephone: (916) 324-4933.

Designing District Evaluation Instruments for Math and Science Process Skills

Contact: Shelley Ann Lipowich, 6321 N. Canon Del Pajaro, Tucson, AZ 85715. Telephone: (602) 299-9583.